ALSO BY KAY BRATT

Wish Me Home
True To Me
No Place too Far
Into the Blue
Silent Tears; A Journey of Hope in a Chinese Orphanage
Chasing China; A Daughter's Quest for Truth
Mei Li and the Wise Laoshi
Eyes Like Mine
The Bridge
A Thread Unbroken
Train to Nowhere
The Palest Ink
A Welcome Misfortune
To Move The World
The Scavenger's Daughters
Tangled Vines
Bitter Winds
Red Skies

ALL (MY) DOGS GO TO HEAVEN

ALL (MY) DOGS GO TO HEAVEN

Kay Bratt

ALL (MY) DOGS GO TO HEAVEN

Do dogs go to Heaven? Do dogs have souls? Both are common questions, especially among those who've lost furry family members and can't bear the thought of never seeing them again.

Kay Bratt explores these ideas in *All (my) Dogs Go to Heaven*. Touching on relevant biblical scriptures, she chronicles her tumultuous past—including a traveling childhood and a near decade of domestic abuse—revealing how her beloved pets helped her cope and instilled hope for better days ahead.

Interspersed within this memoir are short essays from real people who have experienced signs from their departed pets as proof that they are still around in spirit. Included in the back of the book is a grief guide to help get us through those first devastating days after our loss.

Insightful and fascinating, Kay Bratt has ultimately given us a message of hope with *All (my) Dogs Go to Heaven*. –Judy Morgan, Founder of Yorkie Rescue of the Carolinas

DEDICATED TO GRANDPA OLIVER

*my dapper little gentleman who stole
hearts all around the world.*

1

———————

AN UNBEARABLE BURDEN

I s your soul being crushed with grief after losing a pet? Do you feel like you don't know how you will go on without your best friend? I know exactly how you feel, and I want to tell you that, first, it's okay to not be okay. It hurts like hell.

Yes, I'm going to use the words Heaven and Hell on the same page because that's the best description of what we go through when we lose a pet. The greatest mystery of our life is what happens when we die. And for me, the second greatest mystery is where do my pets go when *they* die? And what was the purpose of having them with me throughout my life if only to have to go through this unbearable pain of saying goodbye?

This book will help answer that for me and possibly for you. It is written as the road trip of my life and chronicles how my pets have gotten me through the deepest lows. This book is also a tribute to those animals and a light research into the age-old question...

Do dogs go to Heaven?

Included are contributions from myself and other pet owners who feel that their dogs have sent them signs from the other side. Written from the point of view of a normal person just like you, this book is meant to comfort those of us who have lost pets who, to us, are not just animals but are deeply loved members of our family.

Having a pet is like being a parent. I even hate to use the term *pet*.

They are so much more than that.

We take responsibility for their life, and we strive to cover their physical and emotional needs. Research shows that losing a pet can be just as devastating, and sometimes even more so, as losing a relative. It only makes sense, as our pets love us unconditionally, providing loyalty and affection without expectation of anything in return past the simplicity of food, shelter, and the occasional belly rub. They also don't judge you, criticize you, or refuse to speak to you for months on end like humans tend to do when they get their nose out of joint. They see us at our lowest lows and observe our weaknesses and are there as our biggest cheerleaders when we occasionally get things right in life.

Honestly, it marvels me how some people can live without a dog. Or a cat. Or some kind of pet. Where do they find that unconditional love that we all crave? I feel sorry for their loss of not knowing what it's like to have that special gift.

Last year, I lost one of my fur-kids, and I can tell you without exaggeration that it felt like my world was suddenly dark. It's been months, and there are still days that I grieve deeply and ask myself if I did the right thing by letting him go on to a place of no pain and sickness. Selfishly, I wanted to keep him with me. I'll admit that.

Thankfully, I love him more than I love myself, and I had to give him relief.

His death filled me with guilt and sent me wondering once again if dogs go to Heaven.

Do they have a soul? If so, where is my little man now? Is he around me, or is he waiting somewhere high in the clouds where I can't see him? I just want someone to tell me that yes, he is in Heaven.

If you are thinking that no one truly has the answer to that, you are right. I even asked a few Christian leaders, those who I feel have a legitimate knowledge of what goes on behind the secret curtain.

They were not of any help.

I understand why, though. No one can say that they know, with one hundred percent irrefutable proof, that our dogs will be in Heaven.

That doesn't stop us from trying to figure it out.

Over the last two decades, I've bought dozens of books about the afterlife and Heaven. I'm a self-dubbed research fanatic, both for my work in writing novels, as well as my quest to just know more in general about the mysteries of the universe.

With every book I read on the subject, I first absorb it, and then I begin research to see what is written against the book or the author. I want to read both sides of the argument—do some people just know what's over there? Do these authors have a special gift that I don't have? Or are they, *as they were called in the old days*, charlatans?

As I conducted my research, I also struggled with the fact that I'm a Christian, though I now consider myself more spiritual than religious. My walk with God might not look like yours, and that's fine. However, there are people in the church who say animals don't have souls, which, by the way, crushes me when I hear them say that.

There was a time that I was in church two to three times a week. That time is not now, but I love the old analogy "going to church doesn't make you a Christian any more than standing in a garage makes you a car."

I do believe there's a God. And that one day I'll meet Him in paradise. Because of that, I needed to know for myself what the Bible had to say about animals in Heaven so that I can know if my babies will be there.

My questions resulted in doing the research and combining it with short memoir excerpts of my life, as it connected to how my specific pets brought me through so many trials, that is now this book. I'll warn you now, if you aren't a fan of an author rambling on about their life experiences, then go ahead and shut the cover and ask for a refund. If all I did was spout what I found in the scriptures, it would be an awfully short and boring book. I think of my life as a very long road trip. And I'm inviting you along.

I also need to tell you that the parts of what I am going to share here are not of the rainbows-and-unicorns variety. I'll bare part of my soul to you in the hopes that despite all that I've been through, you'll agree that I'm not a victim.

I'm a survivor.

Now in my fifth decade of going around this planet, I look back and see there is one overall reaching lesson and reason that I got to this place and am with you now sharing a book about dogs going to Heaven. There are a few other contributions included in the narrative of others who feel that their departed dogs have sent them a sign from the other side.

At the end of the book, you'll find some home remedies for nursing your fur-child, as well as my recipe for home-cooked dog food that my pack goes crazy over. You'll also find a grief guide that I hope will help you get through that first brutal week after losing your fur-child.

I hope this book will give you comfort.

As for the big question of whether your dog goes to Heaven or not, it is up to you to look through my research here and determine if you believe.

However, if there is a kernel of wonderment in your

soul and the ability to walk in faith, then keep reading. I will give you my word, which means everything to me, that I won't write anything in this book that I don't myself believe is completely true.

On the other hand, I won't try to convince you of anything.

So, take a seat and buckle up. I'm going to tell you about the dogs I've known in my life, what I have learned, and what *I* believe. The rest is up to you.

2

———————◆———————

MY FACE MAY BE WHITE,
BUT MY HEART IS PURE GOLD

Oliver paced the length of the yard, careful to avoid the low spots of standing water. Rain in the cold temperatures of December were the worst, and he had tired of standing outside the door, hoping to be let in to feel the warmth on his cold, wet feet. His clumsily healed and crooked jaw was proof that it wouldn't benefit him to whine or scratch either. After fourteen long years, the shape of his malnourished body and pus-filled mouth showed that his care was the lowest of priorities for the family inside. He knew what he meant to them, and that his was a sad tale of unrequited love.

Though it pained him to give up, it was well past time. They would never return his loyalty. The pack mom and dad were too busy trying to wrangle the rowdiest of small humans, coming and going at all hours of the day and night, sometimes yelling and causing all sorts of ruckus. There was no room in their lives for a small little man as himself, no matter how well-behaved he believed himself to be. Things were different when he had first come to them, a fluffy and eager-to-please puppy, barely wet behind the ears and with the breath that made them giggle. They didn't have little humans back then and claimed he was their everything.

There were tumbles and hugs, snuggles and smiles, all sprinkled with promises to protect him forever. He believed them and felt he'd found his pack. He pledged to return their devotion and protect them with everything he had.

Then he grew older, no longer able to tumble and play—his breath losing its sweetness. The little humans came, one after the other. Later, a young puppy took his place, and it was the center of attention, making him feel invisible until one day, he was told to just stay outside.

Those first nights he couldn't believe they really meant him to stay out there forever. Surely, they would let him in. He had held up his part of the plan—he still loved and tried to protect them. Why did they suddenly no longer care for his well-being? Still yet, he waited patiently by the door. They would come to their senses. He could teach the young pup how to behave, give her all the advice she needed to be a good dog.

But the door never opened.

At least not for him.

Oliver would not be allowed to rejoin his pack. Didn't they see that dogs weren't loners? It was the worst life sentence you could have, to be cast out and left to spend every waking minute alone, but at least he could count himself lucky that he wasn't sentenced to being tied up or chained to a tree.

They didn't care if he wandered. But he didn't. He waited.

Hoping they would love him again.

The summers were brutal in the humid Georgia temperatures, but the winters—well, they were something else entirely. In the light of the day, being of small stature, he was stalked by the hawks and had to be careful. At night the sounds of coyotes howling sent shivers of fear through him, and he huddled under anything he could find. And oh, the fleas. Even in the coldest of colds, he could not rid himself of the tormenting creatures as they burrowed and bit, depleting the slight reserves he barely had. He'd had to stop obsessing over them, though, because his first priority was simply staying alive.

To lay down and die would not be his legacy.

Now night would soon come again, and his old bones were no longer able to stand the bitter cold rumbling through them as he trembled and waited for the sun to rise.

He also had an epiphany. Someone out there needed him. And he had to find her. Today he would start his journey, and if night came too quickly, he would find somewhere else to sleep, hopefully somewhere safe from the packs that hunted for small creatures like him.

With one more look at the place he had given most of his life to, he headed for the driveway that led out. He would stay low and definitely wouldn't venture onto the pavement. It was a country road without much traffic, but an old dog knew a few things, and one of those things was that you didn't test your courage against five thousand pounds of metal and motor.

He walked at least a mile and then tired and decided to rest.

With a stick in his mouth to gnaw at and ease at least some of his hunger pains, he settled into the high grass of the ditch. As he rested, he listened to the occasional car go by and even heard the sound of a truckload of chickens being transported to the coops of doom. He said a prayer for them, even though they weren't his acquaintances, but other chickens were, and he had said goodbye to many feathered friends over the years.

They'd done their best to teach him to survive, and he could hunt and peck insects with the best of them. He had even conquered the unique chicken noise in the back of his throat and, along with a certain strut, sometimes almost believed he was one of them. He also knew that he carried the deadly stench of the chicken farm, but that was a small price to pay for the bit of companionship he'd found there.

Suddenly he heard another car coming closer, and his ears perked up. Why was this car making his pulse race and his heart leap in joy?

He must take a look.

Slowly, because his old bones ached so very much, he stepped to the top of the road shoulder and peeked out.

The car passed him by, and his heart fell.

He was too late.

Sighing, he turned to go back and rest a bit more before he must remain awake all night to keep guard.

But wait—first he heard the car stop, and then he saw the red lights on its rear shine. They began to back up, straight toward him.

Before they could change their mind, and knowing he was jeopardizing his life, he stepped completely out onto the road in full view.

The car door opened, and a woman stepped out.

"Well, hello. Aren't you a dapper little fellow?" she said softly.

She didn't come closer, and he appreciated her respectful distance. He'd also learned that all humans weren't to be trusted.

"You poor thing. You look like you're starving."

She didn't mention how badly he smelled, and that saved his dignity more than he could ever let her know. Her voice was encouraging and perhaps tinged with a bit of pity. But it was kind, and he knew, yes—he could feel it—she was the one.

"Do you want to come with me, and we can figure out who you belong to?" she asked, kneeling down a few feet away, welcoming him to make the choice.

There really was no indecision on his part. Feeling lighter and happier than he had in years, he found his prance again as he made his way over to her and allowed her to reach down and pick him up. When he felt the gentleness in her touch and the way she cradled him close, despite his unkempt condition, there was no doubt.

She was his epiphany, and whether she knew it or not, she needed him.

Together, they climbed into the car, and he perched on her lap, looking straight out the front window in anticipation that whatever was next would be better than what was.

3

———————•———————

HEY MISTER, LET THAT DOG GO

Many of my readers know of me because of my Bratt Pack and their stories that I share on my social-network platforms. There is something going on all of the time between what happens at home and the many dogs in and out of my life through the rescue I volunteer for. What they may not know is that I have always been a huge lover of animals, especially dogs.

The first dog that I remember was a German shepherd we had when I was around seven years old. At the time, we were living in Kansas and our neighbors had him tied to a clothesline, even in the brutal cold of winter.

The neighbor didn't treat him as member of his family—to him, the dog was just a dog.

Yes, the neighbor was *that* kind of human.

My dad was a young family man of only about twenty-two years old when he witnessed the neighbor kids beating the dog with a stick.

This wasn't an easy situation for my dad, because the neighbor was one of his good buddies. They were both only in their early twenties, and even back then, there was a code between men that you didn't criticize the way your friends did things.

At the time, we were as poor as a church mouse, but

it bothered my dad to see an animal in that kind of situation, so he respectfully asked to pay the dog's ransom. He wasn't asking to buy him, as he knew he couldn't afford to add another mouth to feed, but he thought the dog would have a better chance on his own than being chained to the clothesline.

"I'll give you twenty bucks to let him go," my dad said to the neighbor.

"Nope," said the neighbor. "He's my alarm system."

"Then tell your kids to stop beating him."

"Aww, they ain't hurting him. Just playing around."

"Thirty bucks," my dad said, cringing as the dog took another blow.

The neighbor shook his head. "He'll just run if I let him go."

Dad told me that he played it cool, but he wasn't going to give up. He knew he had fifty bucks to his name, but the neighbor was playing hardball.

"Fifty," Dad finally said, thinking how much my mom was going to kill him. They had three young kids, and even making rent and putting food on the table was a challenge.

That got the neighbor's attention.

Dad pulled together every dollar in his wallet, and the neighbor strode over and released the dog then stood back, waiting for him to bolt.

The dog came straight to my dad.

The rest was history.

Czar (pronounced *Zarr*) was a very special dog. Loving and loyal to a fault, he was calm and didn't think anything of the fact that he'd joined a family who would be traveling all around the states and living in many different homes. As though he'd never known anything different, he was our dog, and we were his people.

Most of my memories with him are from his final home when we lived in Nebraska. We started out there in the tiny town of Odessa, where we knew not a soul, as a family of five with a big dog, all squished into a tiny, shabby motel room.

The majority of the parking lot around the buildings was gravel, and you could pick up a rock, let Czar smell it, and mark it somehow. Then you'd throw it out to fall amongst the thousands of other rocks, and somehow, Czar would find that exact stone and bring it right back to you.

Without any training, he knew how to sit.

Stay.

Speak.

Fart on command.

Oh, oops. Not a great skill to have, but at least Dad had someone else to blame.

I think it was all that cheap canned dog food that, at the time, our family thought was synonymous with feeding him *special* food.

After several months, the manager of the motel took off, and the owner offered my mom the job. They moved us out of that room (thank goodness) and put us up in the main home. All these years, up until last year, I thought it was a nice three-bedroom house. Turns out it was an old two-bedroom double-wide. But from a child's point of view, it was a castle compared to the motel room.

Also, taking a more permanent decision to stay awhile was the catalyst in my walk with God. There was a tiny one-room church a few miles from us that most in town went to. The preacher and his wife, Uncle Pete and Aunt Eula, heard about us living at the motel and came to invite us all to church. My parents passed on the invitation but allowed them to pick us up each Sunday and Wednesday night.

I loved that little church. As young as I was, I fully embraced the discovery that I had a Father who loved me. Those sweet angels also gave us scholarships to attend their church camp, called Camp Joy. Wow—we made some wonderful memories going to that camp.

In the big house (actually, it was tiny) at the motel, my mom took the master bedroom because it was closest to the room on the end that was used as an office. She got up when the bell rang to check in the late-night customers, mostly truck drivers or people on the road who were too poor or too tired to make it to a decent lodging. Oh, but one time we had Donna Fargo's tour bus. Anyone old enough to remember her and her famous songs "Funny Face" or "The Happiest Girl in the Whole USA"? Well, I can tell you, she wasn't happy with Odessa, Nebraska, and her lone option for lodging. To prove that, her crew stayed in the rooms, but she didn't leave the bus. She did, however, sign a poster for my mom. And considering her real name was Yvonne Vaughn, I'm not sure why her needs were so lofty. (Kidding! Fargo Fans, don't send me hate mail!)

Anyway, Donna Fargo was the motel's only claim to fame, but there was a wonderful old (like, really old) truck driver who would eat home-cooked family meals with us when he came through. We tried valiantly to get my grandmother to consider dating him, but she wouldn't do it.

There was also a set of twin brothers named Ronnie and Rannie who came each year to Nebraska for a week of pheasant hunting. My sister and I had little-girl crushes on them, since they were twins, you know. I remember they would save us the prettiest feathers. Of course, now I'd be horrified because I don't believe in hunting only for sport.

In the main house, my father, twin sister, my older brother, and I shared the other bedroom. Dad and my brother were in bunk beds on one wall while my sister and I took the double bed on the other. It was crowded but a mansion compared to the tiny motel room that was used as our entire home.

Czar enjoyed his new job. He took his role as our protector very seriously and would accompany my mom to the office, standing guard as every customer checked in or out. Our loyal guardian was also known to follow me in and out of the house at night as I sleepwalked around. My dad would not wake me, due to his superstitions, and he felt secure that Czar would make sure that nothing would happen to me.

When my youngest sister was born and then became a toddler, she had her own escort as well as she played around the motel parking lot and in the small park. Our noble, furry fellow would never let Misty wander into trouble.

Those protective qualities in our dog made Czar that much more special to my parents. And though Dad loved Czar as much as the rest of us did, there was one thing that Czar did that probably put a burr under my dad's saddle.

Back then, it was common for parents to use the belt (or a stick or wooden spoon) on their children for discipline. I'm not condoning it, and I've never physically disciplined my own kids, so please don't send me letters about it. There are a lot of things parents did back then that they now know was wrong and would never want to pass down to future generations.

Czar didn't believe in it at all and was a staunch advocate of the no-touch discipline.

When the belt would come out, he was so protective that Dad would have to lock him into the bathroom before he started the punishment or find his own dog's teeth around his slinging arm. Even then, Czar would howl and try to find a way out to come to our rescue.

Somehow it made the experiences a little less painful knowing that somewhere in the house, Czar was crying with us. When the punishment was over, we had him there for comfort and to bring a sense of calm back to the family.

Looking back, I really feel like Czar acted like a therapy dog even before there was a label for such. My siblings and I saw a lot of trauma while living in that place, and Czar claimed his duty to be there for all of us, stretching himself thin for every member of the family.

Speaking of crying, after seven or so wonderful years that weren't nearly enough, Czar's health started failing. I can still remember how it felt to lay with him on the floor, my head on his body and my fingers running through his hair as I comforted him. Eventually he began to go blind, and the veterinarian told us he'd be fine, to just not move any furniture around and keep everything as he was used to.

Czar was brave, despite the continuing loss of sight. Slowly and carefully, he was still able to get around inside and out and wouldn't even think of ever having an accident in the house. He had his pride and still wanted to be our protector.

We continued to let him do his business and vigil where he wanted then waited for him to paw at the door when he was ready to come back in.

One day, that pawing never came.

After realizing he hadn't asked to come in, my parents bundled up and went out to try to find him. He wasn't anywhere close like he usually stayed, and over the next few hours, they expanded their search wider until they finally found him behind one wall of the motel building.

Our amazing and majestic boy had taken a long walk to end his life on his own terms. They found him asleep in the snow, and he would never wake again. Throughout ancient times, dogs have served as companions and/or taken their place to work herding sheep, hunting, or being a guardian. I believe that Czar was sent to my family to be a protector, because he performed the role so completely.

God said, "A good man cares for the needs of his animal" (Proverbs 12:10). That establishes that He cares for animals and wants us to do the same. So, if God cares for animals, why wouldn't He want them in Heaven? That wouldn't make sense.

The first family that Czar was with did not care for him or meet his needs. Our family did, and God rewarded us with a loyal dog who only wanted to protect and please.

In the wild, when an animal is sick or about to die, they go off to do it alone, away from the pack as their presence of weakness can bring danger from the outside.

In Czar's last walk, I believe he took himself away from our family for one last gift of protection. What came after discovering Czar had gone from his earthly body was the first memory I have of how loss affected not only us children but also my parents. In my mind, I can still see them holding each other as they sobbed, grieving for the dog that, to them, was never just a dog.

He was family.

4

IN LOVING MEMORY OF CZAR

It is with great sadness that we must memorialize our noble German shepherd, Czar, guardian of four gnarly children against butt-whippings and weird motel customers who chose to stay at his home that was more like a Bates Motel than a Holiday Inn.

Czar took his role as protector very seriously, and he also never met a rock he didn't love and couldn't recognize from a whole parking lot full of other rocks. Czar preferred to sleep on the floor, most frequently behind his pack dad's armchair, where they could pass gas in unison and blame the other.

Preceding Czar in death was his tiny Pomeranian sister, Fulang, who unfortunately thought it was safe to taunt and eat out of the bowl of her larger brother and lost an eye over it. They are now together and once again fighting over a bowl of cheap dog food.

In lieu of flowers, please contact your local animal control and thank them for being the angels of dogs tied out on chains, left in the weather to freeze, or to die of sweltering temps. All dogs should be cared for and treated with respect, and Czar was a fine example of forgiveness in the face of human failure.

Not Czar, but as close as I could find.

5

DOODLE DEXTER FULL OF LOVE

By Laurie, neuroscientist/neuropsychologist, skeptic, and dog lover

While doing research into this phenomenon, or gift—*whatever you decide to call it*—I stumbled across a story posted online by a woman named Laurie. I sent her a message and asked if I could interview her by phone and, depending on how that went, possibly use her story in this book. I didn't want to commit, because if I felt like she was a total fruitcake, or her story was just fantastical wishes, I knew I would not use it. There are plenty of those out there, and being the cynic I am, I only want to be involved with the stories I feel are plausible and coming from someone I would not doubt.

The call and interview went well.

Here is her story.

Laurie is a neuroscientist/neuropsychologist who has done brain research at MGH Harvard University and MIT. As she relayed to me, in her scientific field of study, she has been trained to question everything and is aware of the mental biases and tricks one can unknowingly play on themselves. All of that is to me what makes her story so special, as well as the fact that she was so convinced of what was happening that she felt she had to share it with those of you who, like her, have been dealt a devastating loss.

Laurie was all set to receive one of the first miniature doodles in the country back when the breed was brand-new. Instead, when she showed up to the airport, she met one of the biggest puppies she'd ever seen, weighing in at thirty pounds at just ten weeks. Not what she was expecting, but he stole her heart anyway.

Let's talk about a big fluffy boy that was Laurie's best friend and the sole love of her life before he agreeably decided to share the spotlight with her husband, Jim.

Dexter and his pack mom shared an amazing relationship and strong bond, even after she married. Laurie gave Dexter a life that many dogs could only dream of—frequent trips to the park, long hikes, even sledding together down the steep hills of snow. Dexter also liked water, being near it, in it, or on top of it with her as she skimmed across the surface in her kayak.

In return, he was the best companion she could've ever asked for. Loyal, loving, fun, and adventurous. It was like Dexter was put on this Earth exactly for her. For ten long years that were still much too short, Laurie and Dexter were together every chance they could get.

Then Dexter got sick with hemangiosarcoma, cancer of the blood.

While he was being treated at Angel Memorial, all the people whose lives had been touched by this remarkable soul were worried. The veterinarians there told Laurie that they had never seen a dog get so many visitors before.

If love could've kept him alive, you wouldn't be reading this now.

When Dexter died, Laurie was devastated and lost without him. It was too hard to understand how a dog with so much life and love could just be there one day then gone the next.

The day after he died, Laurie was at home, feeling depressed and lonely. She was startled when her key finder began to go off, for no reason. She thought nothing of it until she went to the park that she and Dexter used to go to together. She sat on a bench by the water fountain and was thinking of him, and the key finder went off again. For Laurie, it was confusing, and she wanted to believe it was a sign from her dog, that he was still with her, but she still wasn't sure what to think. Could that even be possible? She decided not to think too much about it and just tried to work through her grief.

However, over the next few weeks, different key finders they owned, depending on which one was near, would go off at random times but only when visiting a place that was special to both her and Dexter. She and Jim at first thought perhaps it was the batteries in the key finder, or perhaps it was broken. They changed batteries and confirmed the key finders were fine, and they would still go off, even with fresh batteries.

Laurie began to let herself believe it was indeed Dexter, sending her a sign that he was fine and was still around her.

Then in August, the signs from Dexter completely stopped.

As the months passed, Laurie waited to hear from Dexter again. She watched the key finders, trying to will them to go off again. But nothing.

The silence saddened her, and she wondered if it was all just a huge coincidence.

When December crept up, Laurie decided to ask Dexter—or God or whomever was out there—to give her another message, if indeed it had been Dexter. This time, she got specific and asked that the key finder go off on her dog's upcoming birthday, December 20, or on Christmas Day as a holiday gift to her that could once and for all tell her that it was him, and that he was not truly gone forever.

Nothing happened leading up to the day of the twentieth, and Laurie was sure she'd never hear from him again. When his birthday rolled around, her brother visited, and they spent hours shopping for Christmas and driving around town.

Throughout the day, they talked of Dexter and how much he was missed. Laurie reminded her brother that it was Dexter's birthday and confessed she had hoped to hear from him because nothing had happened for the last four months.

As the day was coming to a close, they finished shopping and went to the dog park that Dexter loved.

As soon as they pulled up, the key finder began going off.

Laurie turned to her brother, lost for words, and they both smiled.

The key finder continued to go off and on several times throughout the next ten or so minutes, and Laurie was thrilled that she had gotten her wish for Dexter's birthday.

Laurie was happy with the signs, and she didn't want to be greedy, so she didn't ask again. However, Christmas Day rolled around, and just as she was getting herself ready to go sledding outside, in Dexter's honor, the key finder went off.

She remembered that she'd also asked for a sign on Christmas Day. Dexter had waited five days between the last sign so that he could give it to her on the very day she'd asked for it. Laurie was ecstatic and shocked, and many emotions all poured together.

After Christmas passed, things were quiet for a while until Laurie traveled to Arizona to celebrate her own birthday with her parents. The night before her birthday, she knew she didn't have a key finder with her, so she prayed that the next day, her husband's key finder would go off as a sign from Dexter. Laurie kept her plea to herself and didn't even tell Jim, who was still back in Ontario, thinking this would be the ultimate test.

The very next day, Laurie was enjoying a moment with her parents when her phone went off to tell her she had a text message.

Babe, the key finder has been going off like crazy all morning. I heard a clicking and thought my car was acting up then realized it was the key finder.

Laurie was speechless.

Jim was thousands of miles away, and his key finder hadn't made a peep in more than three months. How could it be a coincidence? It was the most amazing birthday present she could've received.

After her birthday, the messages were silent or, at least, the key finders were. One afternoon, Laurie was sitting outside. A friend had given her a statue that resembled Dexter, and Laurie got up and went to it then put her hand on its head.

"You would've loved this place, boy," she said, looking out over the water.

Her gaze was drawn to some extraordinary clouds building over to her right, so she walked through the trees to get a better look then snapped a handful of shots. It wasn't until after she walked away and sat back down to look through the photos that she realized a few of them had a shape that appeared to look exactly like the back of her beloved boy's head.

Had Dexter been right there, thinking of her as she was thinking of him? I believe the picture tells the tale.

As the anniversary of Dexter's death approached, Laurie still wasn't over his loss and needed just one more sign. She prayed she would hear from him on the date of his passing, August 9.

It had been six months since her birthday and his last sign, so she knew it was a long shot, but on August 6, the key finder rang out. Then it did it again on August 7.

But it was silent on August 8.

Laurie thought that would be the end of it. On August 9, the anniversary of Dexter's death, Laurie took off on a hike to a place she used to go with him. As she walked, she thought of him and what a good boy he was—just a gentle giant full of love and loyalty. Her heart ached again with the missing of his constant presence, and then the key finder went off.

She stopped and stared at the key finder, willing it to give her an answer.

Was she losing her mind?

Perhaps it had all been just a giant coincidence, and there was no way possible a dog could send signs from the other side. She began to cry, knowing that if that was the case, her dog was gone forever and had not been around her at all since the day of his death a year before.

She began to walk, but she cried as she went. Dexter was gone. She'd never see him again, and her mind was just playing tricks on her.

Suddenly, the key finder in her pocket went off.

She stopped walking and pulled it out and looked at it.

Did I make this up? she thought.

Then it went off again.

And again and again.

Laurie laughed through the tears that ran down her face. Joy and peace filled her heart more than it had with any other of the signs. This time, she was sure.

Okay, Dexter. I get it.

You are with me.

Laurie never doubted again, and the messages stopped.

I feel that her dog got his point across, and because her heart was no longer broken, Dexter's work was done.

God created animals before he created man, and only because they gave him delight. Man was created later and was given dominion over animals. Don't forget that God also commands us to care for our animals, and because he delights in them, it goes without saying that those who are cruel to animals will have to answer for their deeds. Because of Job 12, "but ask the animals, and they will teach you," it is clear to me that God wants us to observe and pick up the best traits from animals. Dogs (and other pets) are loyal, hardworking, and forgiving. They do not hold grudges, nor do they have evil thoughts.

Most of all, dogs represent love and devotion, and God wants nothing but for us all to love each other.

6

IN LOVING MEMORY OF DEXTER

Dexter the Doodle passed away peacefully in his mom's arms after ten and a half years of living life to its fullest and making friends wherever he went. Born December 20, Dexter was thirty pounds at just ten weeks, was either the biggest miniature puppy ever bred or was the product of a miscommunication.

However it went, Dexter used his big paws and even bigger personality to win hearts and teach those around him that negativity does not have a place in this world, and instead, you should go and embrace all it has to offer. Some of his favorite things were big hugs, long hikes, sledding down hills, swimming, and kayaking across the lake.

In lieu of flowers, Dexter would want you to go to the lake, jump in then out, shake off, then do it all again. Dexter left a legacy of inclusivity, being kind to everyone in his path, purebred or not. In his later years, Dexter stopped worrying about whether he was a golden or a poodle and embraced his quirky individual personality. Many of his lifetime fans are relieved that as a reward for a life well lived, Dexter is safe and happy and has finally figured out just who is a good boy.

THOU SHALT COVET
YOUR NEIGHBOR'S DOG

A few years after Czar passed on, our family moved again. Then again. And then once more before landing in a little rented farmhouse between Odessa and Kearney, Nebraska. As far as rentals went, it wasn't anything fancy, but it was clean, and it began as a good place to make memories.

When you first walked into the door of the house, you came into a small kitchen that led into an even smaller living room. Next to it, I remember my brother had a makeshift room that we had to pass through to get to the room my twin sister and I shared. His door was only tacked-up sheets between his room and the living room, and between his room and our bedroom. He would fuss when we'd come through and *bother* him (as though we could magically transport ourselves to our room without going through his).

I'm fairly sure my brother's room was supposed to be a small dining room, but I couldn't swear to it. I cannot remember my younger sister having a room, so I think she slept with my parents in the back of the house.

Thinking of that house brings back a lot of memories of being cold.

Inside and outside.

Probably why these days I can't get enough hot baths and warm socks, even in the warm climate I now live in. It all, as they say, is in my head.

Despite remembering being cold all the time, our family was doing better by then, a fact I know must be true because I'm sure my dad had a new truck when we lived there.

Both of my parents worked for the same Chevrolet dealership, mostly doing lot duty and detailing cars, but it was regular income and, from what I'm guessing, much more than they'd made when we lived at the motel. They worked long hours, but when they came home, my mom always made a good, hot meal for the family, then my sister and I would do the cleanup as she headed to bed early. At that house, Mom was twenty-eight years old with four kids and a really hard full-time job in the cold winters of Nebraska.

Yep, I'm sure she was tired. And yep, my mom is made of steel. She's not one who is going to bake cookies and read you a bedtime story or whisper words of affection and kiss you good night, but she worked her fingers to the bone to make sure we ate and had a roof over our heads.

That is just who she was.

I was ten years old when we moved to the farmhouse, and one afternoon, I noticed the tiniest baby mouse in the kitchen. No bigger than my pinkie, it was still in the baby stage, all fur and twitching whiskers. I was mesmerized, as was my sister and brother when I called them to see.

I'll never forget the shrieking my mother did when she came home from work and we'd pulled every drinking glass from the cupboard and covered about a dozen baby mice with them as they ran out from under the stove. I thought my mother would skin us alive, and until then, I did not know she has such a fear of rodents.

Amusingly, I had my own shriek-fest as an adult years later when one evening, I opened my nightstand drawer (in a brand-new house) to see a mouse staring up at me. I screamed bloody murder, and the mouse jumped straight up into the air, causing me to scream again. Then it took off, and I never saw it again. I felt my mother's pain in that moment and understood why I was lucky she hadn't beaten me to death when I'd started my own mouse nursery back in that farmhouse.

The farmhouse was quaint, but my favorite part of living there was that the property had so many places that I could take my bag of books and disappear to. Our landlord lived in a big farmhouse just up the road, and she kept her white Eskimo dog in a kennel outside.

Her name was Ms. Charlotte, and she'd let me or my siblings come take Sam for a walk whenever we wanted to. We all loved that dog so much, and we loved her too. Because we rarely got to see our own grandmothers, she was a sort of stand-in and would give us cookies and milk and hover over us.

My twin sister, brother, and I were home alone a lot while my parents worked, and I think Ms. Charlotte felt sorry for us and was glad to have a nice little family living in her rental with children she could bake for who walked her dog.

I spent a lot of time alone on that farm property without my siblings around too.

That was the first time that we could all go find our own corners outside to have some privacy. We had a bookmobile that would come around like clockwork, and I loved getting my pack of books and climbing into the hayloft in the barn or even up what felt like a palace of haystacks and then burrowing in so no one could see me.

I'd stay gone for hours on the weekend and was never called in by my parents as long as I was in the door by dinnertime. I can imagine for them the place was truly a paradise to be able to send three of your four kids out the door and have some peace and quiet.

My parents were painfully young and could've easily let someone else take us and been free of the hard responsibilities. I give them credit that they never did. But don't think they didn't threaten it. Also, in our family, words or touches of affection just weren't a thing. You did what you were told when you were told to do it. It was a hard life, but at that time, it was speckled with little touches of joy that included walks with Sam and hours of time to read.

My sister and I had a best friend named Tracy who went to school with us there. One afternoon, she came home from school with us, and after chores, we were going to cross the highway to go explore an abandoned old house rumored to be haunted. We weren't supposed to be crossing the highway without permission.

And we would face the ultimate consequences.

Tracy, this wonderful and beautiful girl that everyone loved, ran out in front of an oncoming car. My brother was already on the other side of the road, and my sister and I hadn't yet left our side, and that left nowhere for the driver to go to avoid hitting Tracy.

I remember her hesitating as she looked, but by that time, there was a truck coming from the other direction, and she couldn't retreat. She only paused for half a second, and she nearly made it to the other side. She was only one small step away.

The memory of the moment of impact and every detail is etched in my mind forever. There was a sound I never want to hear again, just before her body flew into the air and began a spiraling descent.

My twelve-year-old brother desperately tried to catch her as she came back down.

He didn't.

And to this day, he can't talk about it.

Also, to this day, the three of us have never brought it up together.

The pain and guilt are too deep.

As an adult, I know it was not our fault, but the child in me thought it was, and somewhere inside, she is still there, traumatized and sorry.

Back at the scene, while my brother and sister took off screaming, I knelt on the highway beside Tracy, begging her to get up and stop playing around, refusing to acknowledge the blood that flowed from her ears and mouth and the fact that she was not communicating.

First, another friend's mother stopped and kept Tracy alive until the ambulance came. I blacked out that memory, but soon after, I found myself standing in Ms. Charlotte's kitchen. I was told to call Tracy's family, and after I did, I went back into the cold.

Somehow, the dog, Sam, knew something terrible had happened, and when I passed his kennel, instead of his usual eagerness and tail-wagging for attention, he somberly came to the fencing to lick my hand in silent sympathy.

At barely eleven years old, I found the walk down that dirt road back to my own little home was the longest walk of my life.

I was terrified at what would happen to my best friend.

ALL (MY) DOGS GO TO HEAVEN 33

And horrified that the accident had happened because she came to see me.

Tracy died of massive head injuries only a few hours after arriving at the hospital.

Because of a mix-up of communication and the fact that Tracy and I had traded coats that afternoon, my parents thought it was me that was struck, and they dashed to the hospital, terrified at what they'd find.

When they made it home that night, the door slammed open, and I flinched as my father strode in to find us. I expected to get the worst spanking I'd ever had, for making choices that killed our friend.

Instead, my father gathered my sister and me into his arms and sobbed in relief that it wasn't one of his children who were taken.

When we returned to our tiny one-room school, our friends decided they would not have anything to do with us and called us murderers, shunning us in every activity and chance they could.

My teacher took me aside and told me she wanted me to write out everything that happened the afternoon that Tracy lost her life. That was my first exercise in writing as therapy, and she took the six-page story of tragic details along with my sketched diagram of the scene, and I never saw it again.

We didn't tell our parents about our school woes. That wasn't the kind of family we were. Our best friend was dead because we went somewhere we shouldn't have gone, and we were meant to suck it up and deal with the consequences. Our parents' lives were full of hard work and heartache, and they didn't complain.

We were expected to be the same.

That wasn't the only problem we had, though. Eventually we would have to tell them one of the aftermath issues we were having.

Tracy's father, who before the accident had never

wanted anything to do with us other than a passing hello when we played at their house, suddenly started showing up at our school and taking us home with him, without permission. The ride to their farm was always somber, and he barely spoke. We didn't even feel like we knew him.

Once there, he'd give us popsicles and lean against the counter to stare at us in his kitchen, saying that we brought back memories of Tracy for him. Then he'd fall into deafening silence before finally taking us home and dropping us off, not a word said on the ride.

My sister and I didn't ever want to go with him, but we also didn't want to hurt his feelings. His daughter was gone forever because she came to our home. And he was an adult. So we did what we were told, though I only wanted to come home and be with Sam or be left alone to disappear between the pages of my books.

Sam was always the first choice, though. He brought me comfort that no one else offered, a gift that I can't imagine now how I would've gotten through those first dark days without.

Dogs are amazing like that, aren't they?

The impromptu meetings with Tracy's dad continued for a while.

The popsicles.

The silent stares.

My father would finally step in after a few ignored warnings and demand Tracy's dad leave us alone. Then we moved away.

But I could never outrun the guilt. Or the fear of being anywhere near a highway. Or the nightmares and dreams of Tracy.

Years later as an adult, while my mom was in the car and I was talking about my uncontrollable fear that my children would die from being struck down on a highway, I mentioned to my mom about continually reliving every detail of the accident.

I told her that the grief and dreams never left me and how I think not allowing us to attend Tracy's funeral made it even harder for us to have closure. I spoke of the recurring nightmares that went from Tracy being struck over and over, to my own children being the victims.

She thought for a moment, and I held my breath.

With her head turned to look out the passenger window, she said, "Yes, I used to hear you girls crying in your sleep. I guess I should've taken you to therapy or something."

My mother was only twenty-eight years old when the accident happened, and at that time, she was consumed with just getting by and supporting her four children. I'm sure she was devastated for Tracy and her family, and likely, she didn't know how to approach our own trauma either. As she handled everything else in her life, she must have felt it was best not to discuss it and instead just move on with the hard business of merely surviving.

In the car with me last year, when she admitted to hearing us cry in the night, it was the end of the first and only time we ever talked about Tracy's accident, but for me, I was never able to move on.

7

IN LOVING MEMORY OF SAM

It is with sadness that we announce the passing of the loving dog, Sam, who has been gone at least nigh on thirty years or more but remains in the memory of three forever-traumatized children.

Sam was an old but good dog who filled a lonely place in the hearts of the little humans who lived on his property and liked to put their hands through the metal wires of his cage in an attempt at more sloppy kisses. On long walks around the farm and through the pasture, Sam behaved like a perfect gentleman, trotting along in his happiness to be freed from his solitary abode for however long he could manage.

Sam would want children everywhere to feel loved and appreciated, especially at times they cannot feel it from anyone else.

Rest in peace, you beautiful boy, Sam. In lieu of flowers, please send thoughts of bravery and perseverance to your fellow humans who spend their lives trying to free dogs from lonely backyard kennels.

8

———◆———

ZOE, MY FURRY SOUL MATE
by Tammy Grace, Dog Mom and
USA Today Bestselling Author

Z oe, a beautiful golden retriever, was my furry soul
mate. She was a true gift and an actual gift—my
son gave her to me for Mother's Day. He had left home
and was finishing college and knew that our nest was
empty, and I had been thinking about getting a dog but
had held off because of my grueling work schedule and
the heartbreak of losing my previous dog years ago.

Once I held the sweet golden puppy, who cried most
of the way home, the grief that held me back melted, as
did my heart. Zoe was the sweetest puppy and became a
huge part of our life and family. She loved everyone and
knew to be gentle with my grandma but also enjoyed
a good play fight or tug-of-war. She loved my parents,
giving us hours of laughter watching her prance and
play in their yard.

When I retired, she became my faithful writing buddy,
nestled in my office as I tapped out words on my keyboard. She was such a big part of my life, I included her
in my very first book, and she was the inspiration for
the dogs I featured in the dozens of subsequent stories
I've written. We went on long walks, most days five to

seven miles, and I spoke to her throughout the day and believed she understood every word. She had the most expressive eyes and was my constant companion, who quickly became my best friend for the almost ten years she lived.

She loved to romp in the leaves, and I remember the gorgeous day in November when she started sneezing while we were in the yard. I suspected something was wrong, and our longtime vet was out of the country. The other doctor couldn't find anything and assured me it was nothing, but deep inside, I knew differently and sought out another opinion. Unlike most goldens, she didn't like to travel, and taking her to a clinic out of town was torture for her and us, but we finally got our answer—the news I didn't want and feared most.

Knowing her time was short, I took her to the park each day and tried to do all the things she enjoyed most. The kind vet who diagnosed Zoe told us we would know when it was time to let her go, and when the day came in late February, I wasn't sure I would survive it. Zoe definitely blessed me with the best days and the absolute worst day. I remember holding her collar and rubbing her tags between my fingers, hoping we had done the right thing. When we came home, numb with grief, we boxed up all her toys, beds, bowls, her collar, everything. I couldn't bear to look at any of it.

That night and every night after for months, I heard her coming down the hallway to our room. The click of her nails on the wooden floor, the jingle of her tags on her collar, I actually heard it. I got out of bed more than once, so excited, because I thought maybe, just maybe, it had all been a bad dream.

Without my writing buddy, I wasn't sure I could write. I was working on *A Dog's Hope* at the time and now realize I had poured my emotions, including the profound love I had for Zoe and the unbearable grief at her loss, into those pages. Buddy is the dog in that book, and I was thankful he was a male dog so I could pretend to distance myself a bit, but in essence, Zoe is Buddy.

For months, I kept finding little reminders of Zoe in the house—a ball or a toy I was certain we had stored would show up in a corner. When I cleaned the floors, I would still collect her golden fur, and sometimes it would bring me to tears. The noise of her each night and signs that delivered memories of her stayed with me for months. When they disappeared, I thought that was her way of telling me I would be okay without her, and that she had stayed long enough to let me grieve and heal. Now, I like to think of her with my grandpa, who loved dogs and, like her, thought the best water came right from the hose.

I have a new golden now, and she is vastly different than Zoe. I struggled when we first brought home Izzy, our new puppy, because she wasn't like Zoe. I think I foolishly thought I'd be able to slip right back into the same role and have the same relationship and feelings I had for Zoe, but it wasn't the same. I knew Zoe was special and was a gift that I needed at the right time in my life, but until then, I never realized she was my true furry soul mate. There will never be another like her, but she lives on in all my books, which brings me both sadness and joy.

Dogs don't live long enough to suit me, and I'm not sure I'll ever get over losing Zoe, but despite my fear for the future, our home is filled once again with golden hair and the click of nails on our wooden floors. We often tell Izzy her sister would have loved her, and I hope Zoe knows how much she meant to me. A beautiful drawing of Zoe graces the wall next to my desk, where she still inspires me. Izzy has some big paws to fill, but as I look down from typing this, she is snuggled next to me in the same spot Zoe favored and is quickly becoming my new best friend.

*Submitted by Tammy Grace, Dog Mom and USA Today Bestselling Author

Zoe's mom, Tammy L. Grace, is the USA Today bestselling author of twenty books, including *A Dog's Hope*, written using her pen name, Casey Wilson. You can find out more about her and her books at www.tammylgrace.com.

9

PRAISE YOU IN THIS STORM

As the years went by, we lived in many more small towns. From my humble beginnings in Kansas, we hopped to homes in small towns in Washington State, California, Idaho, back to Kansas, then Oklahoma, Nebraska, Louisiana, back to Nebraska, and then South Carolina.

Whew! That's a lot of traveling around, isn't it? We lived in multiple places within some of those states too. Some of the moves were done across country with two of my siblings and me sleeping in the back of an old truck under a camper top, which we thought was pretty awesome but sure wouldn't be allowed these days.

My parents told the story of one time when they had us on the road, and as usual, they were strapped for money. Off in the distance one day, my dad spotted an old farm and pulled over on the side of the road.

He popped the hood of the car to make it look like we had car trouble, then he snuck off down to the farm and into a watermelon patch to get the family a road snack.

In the meantime, a highway patrol car pulled behind our vehicle, and an officer got out and approached my mom's open window. Across the field, my dad saw what was going on and dropped the goods then raced back toward the car.

"What's going on here?" the officer asked my mom.

Before she could answer, my brother (only five or so years old) popped up and said, "My daddy's stealing us a watermelon!"

Just then, my dad came up out of the ditch. He said the officer turned to look at him.

"Having some car trouble, eh?"

Dad nodded. "Yeah, but she's cooled down. I think we're good to go now."

The officer looked my dad up and down then back into the car and at the three of us sitting wide-eyed in the back seat. "Well, that's a good thing. We wouldn't want old Mister Johnson to think you were wandering around down there in his garden, now would we?"

"No, sir," Dad said, perspiration dotting his upper lip.

"Have a good day, then." The officer nodded then headed back to his car.

Mom said that as we were driving off, Dad gritted his teeth and didn't say a word.

There was another time that we were all stranded in the car during a winter blizzard, and a patrol officer approached the car and told us to get to a motel before our gas ran out.

My dad told him he didn't have the money for lodging. The officer said he'd better find it, or children services were going to be along shortly to get his kids.

Somehow, they scraped it up, though only God knows how.

Despite the many angels who came our way, there were a lot of struggles in the kind of traveling life we led, especially always being the new kid. Luckily, I had a twin sister, so it was like having a best friend travel around the country with me, at least when we weren't ready to kill each other.

On the last family move, we landed in South Carolina

when I was fifteen years old. I remember being rather upset with my dad for taking us from our friends and the last town that we'd loved. That first year was not good. But knowing what I know now, by then I had only sampled the tip of the trauma iceberg for what my life would soon become.

But I'm getting ahead of myself.

In our new town, it wasn't easy to come into the school as a teenager, for either myself or my sister. At our age, friend groups were already built. Adding to that, in the south, the majority of the time, solid friendships are accumulated from growing up together and are far too close-knit to allow new kids into their circles. My sister had been breaking away from our twinship for a few years, wanting to be individuals with separate lives.

The only bright spot I saw was that, for the first time in more than a decade or more, we were going to live close to family. I actually didn't remember ever living close to any relatives. This was an aunt and uncle we had never met, but I'd always wondered what it would feel like to have relatives close enough to visit on a Sunday afternoon.

We did visit them, sparingly and not for any meals. It wasn't the picture-book family get-togethers I had imagined.

Unfortunately, at the time, our parents' relationship was crumbling even more than it ever had, their arguments on another level of madness with all the stress of starting completely over in a new state. Our teenaged brother had decided to stay behind in Nebraska with his pregnant girlfriend, but it was still stressful for my parents to care for a family of five without having a job or soft landing.

From selling most of their belongings before coming, they had enough to get us into a modest little brick-house rental in a decent neighborhood. However, once we got in and settled, a storm came along and knocked a heavy limb onto the power line above our home. That sent a bolt of charge into the house, and the surge took out everything that was electrical. Our television, stereo, curling irons—even the refrigerator was gone for good.

Nothing we owned was worth much, but it then became worthless.

It seemed that bad luck was following us.

It happened in wintertime, and I remember that for several weeks, we kept our food outside in a portable cooler like you'd carry to the beach. Finally, the church (of which we didn't go to) came together and got us a new refrigerator and a bit of money to help replace some of the lost items.

Most of my memories in that little house involve my walks down to a small pond where I would take books to read and my notebook to write letters back home or compose poetry.

By then, my sister had made a new best friend, and I spent most of my time alone. When I was at home, I felt invisible and as though no one cared whether I was there or not.

I was as lonely as a teen could be.

Soon thereafter, our aunt was able to secure my mom a job at a tire-making facility. My father started up his own landscaping business to begin with, but things really looked up for me when our aunt gave us a dog she had found outside a tiny hole-in-the-wall bar called Charlie and Ethels.

Just a mutt—as my dad declared—this dog was found with what appeared to be her brother from the same litter. They were young, skinny, and very hungry, which had brought them to hang out at the back door of the bar.

My aunt was a huge dog lover with five healthy Chinese pugs of her own who we thought were overly spoiled because all of their meals were from home-cooked people food.

Aunt Lee wasn't much too fond of people, and to tell you the truth, I was a little afraid of her. She was a tough old broad, and to me, she always seemed quite surly. In the visits to her home, I never saw her and her husband speak a word to each other, but to her credit, she would never pass by an abandoned dog. She always stopped to rescue them and make sure they found good homes.

It took some convincing for my dad, but Ethel came to be ours while her brother went to another family. Honestly, Ethel wasn't anything to look at, and in the beauty pageant of dogs, she may have been kicked off the stage, but to me, she was perfect.

In Ethel, I found the friend I so badly needed, the comfort my heart searched for in a home that was tumultuous and shaky.

Unlike with Czar, our dad didn't have a fondness for Ethel, and at first, he wouldn't let her come inside. Because of that, I suddenly became quite the outside teenager. I remember a few bad thunderstorms that I sat on the porch, hugging Ethel as, together, we braved through the lightning and thunder. There was something in me that just could not make me leave her out there to brave it alone.

Finally, after a few months of Ethel proving what a good girl she was, she was allowed inside the house. She was not, however, allowed to be on the furniture.

In our bedroom with the door shut, my sister and I would let her on our beds.

Ethel never wanted to be sent outside to live again, so being the smart little cookie she was, when she would hear my dad's footsteps coming up the hall, she would quietly jump down and hide under the bed until he retreated.

During the time we had Ethel, my dad got my little

sister a Pekinese puppy. Her dog was allowed in the house and full prancing permissions all over anything and everything. It was a cute pup, and my dad fell in love with him as much as we all did.

Unfortunately, someone wasn't watching, and the dog ran out and got run down by a car.

One weekend, my sister wanted to go out with some friends and could only get permission if I went along. They always considered me the goody-two-shoes of the pack, and Dad said if I didn't go, she couldn't go.

To tell you the truth, I wasn't that thrilled about going, but I did, for her.

That night I met a guy.

And he was trouble.

A few months later, I decided I was tired of being invisible, and I ran away from home, straight into the arms of the guy that, truth be told, I didn't really even like much. I chose him because he was the only human in my life that showed any interest in me.

Do you want to know the worst thing about that little incident? I forgot my toothbrush and had to use my finger to clean my teeth.

Okay—maybe that isn't the worst thing, but it was traumatic enough that I still remember it, and I've never again forgotten my toothbrush when leaving my home.

I joke to mask the pain, but if you want to know the truth, the worst thing was that for three days and nights, no one cared that I had left.

My parents didn't look for me. They didn't even call the police.

On the fourth day of my escape (of which I was miserable and wished I could go home but was too proud to ask my boyfriend to take me), my sister's friend called my dad and told him where I was.

It was another town about thirty miles from home.

Dad came to pick me up, and the ride back home was

silent.

It had been a long time since the belt had been across my backside, but those memories don't fade, and I knew what I was facing.

When he pulled back into the driveway, Dad got out, and I stayed behind then quickly locked the car doors. My little sister came out onto the porch, and I yelled at her to get our mom, as I thought she might buffer a little of my dad's rage before it poured out onto me.

Only when my mom was dragged out of a dead sleep and staggered outside did I come out of the car and go inside.

I was smart enough to know that I had it coming. I just hoped it wasn't going to be too bad. Well, I shouldn't have been afraid of my dad that time, because as soon as I walked into the house, my mother was waiting. She approached and swung her arm back and hit me across the face so hard that I stumbled across the room.

"You've been out *whoring around!*" she screamed.

Well, he was the only boy I had ever dated, but yes, I had slept with him. Although I was then the same age she was when she'd run away with and then married my father at the insistence of *her mother*, I probably deserved what I got.

My mom doled out the only punishment that day, leaving a physical mark that would stay for a solid week and an emotional scar that I will always carry.

Ethel, however, was thrilled when I returned home, and she alone dried the tears that rained down my face as I lay in my bed that first night, holding the side of my throbbing head as I asked God why I was part of such a dysfunctional family.

Less than a year later, after an intense period of escalated arguments, my mother would ask for a divorce and move into an apartment with us three kids. I was devastated when Ethel was handed back over to my aunt, though I was thankful she had been there for my first hard year in a new place.

After that, everything changed.

Again.

This time, it was different. Before, during all of our moves and changes, the one thing we could depend on was that we would remain a family unit. However, my mom would begin her new life as a single parent, and my father would leave the state for places unknown, and the strict rules and shaky-as-it-was structure of our life would not hold up.

In the midst of our family falling apart, my sister and I lost another best friend in a fiery crash. The car she was in wrapped around a pole as she screamed for someone to get her out before she burned to death. It was such a deep, dark tragedy that involved a driver under the influence, and though we weren't there, it's yet another scene etched into my brain.

It seemed that tragedy followed us, wherever we went.

A short few months later, at only sixteen, I felt invisible again.

I felt like no one cared whether I was there or not. I rarely saw my mom as the foundation of our family crumbled beneath us, sending all of us grasping for whatever life raft we could.

And that boy I ran away with? We started seeing each other again. He didn't go to school but would wait for me to come out of the building and be furious if he caught me talking to anyone. He wanted to rule over every aspect of my life, and unfortunately, I wasn't strong enough to resist it. In my immaturity, I took his obsession for devotion.

Despite my good grades and love for learning, I did as he demanded, and I dropped out of school. That young man would go from an overly jealous and possessive boyfriend to being my legal husband and my abuser and tormenter for the next seven years.

Our wedding night was spent with me in the bedroom crying after he exploded when I dared to interrupt the basketball game on television to suggest going out for a celebratory meal.

I wish someone had stopped me before I embarked on that new phase of my life. But at least I remembered my toothbrush.

10

IN LOVING MEMORY OF ETHEL MAE

Ethel Mae, a square-shaped dog of the Heinz 57 variety, passed away mysteriously and in an unknown location after spending her golden years in the last of many homes around South Carolina. Ethel had somewhat of a vagabond life and was known to visit a dive or two before finding her place and is preceded in death by her twin brother, Charlie.

Ethel was known for her intelligence but also her loyalty and capacity to soothe the hearts of teenagers in a tumultuous home environment. Ethel enjoyed sleeping on beds or under them, depending on who was walking her way, and was smart enough to know the best time to disappear.

In memorial, the family of Ethel Mae would like donations of toys and beds to be delivered to your local shelter or animal rescue.

11

MAKITA

Makita, my best friend, therapist, and love bug
I felt you on the bed last night
It woke me
I was for a brief minute happy and warm inside
I felt you there
When I moved my legs to feel your body
The bed was cold
Reality came quick
I lay wide awake but afraid to move
The pain and loss are unbearable
Thoughts of yesteryear come rushing in
All I want to do is scream

Dear Makita,
My best friend, therapist, and love bug
I lay clutching your lovie
I long to be strong for you
Because I promised I'd be okay
Tears will flow and flow and flow
I will remember the good times
Letting you go was the kindest thing
Being with you at the end was an honor
A tribute to how loved you are

I must conquer fears inside my head
You will never be replaced
Or forgotten

Dear Makita,
My best friend, therapist, and love bug
Today I lit a candle for you
I spoke to your picture in my usual way
I sat down and asked for a sign
The night came, dark and quiet
I heard you, Makita
The familiar sound of your breath as she slept
Close enough to touch but afraid to try
I listened and I know
It was you in sweet slumber
Where you always lay
Through my tears I whispered
I hear you, Makita

When I told your dad
He said he heard you too
It feels strange
And surreal
But comforting too
Your spirit is welcome to visit us
But run free and roam, my Makita
My best friend, therapist, and love bug

Signed, Mom to Makita, Yvonne S.

12

———◆———

IN LOVING MEMORY OF MAKITA

It is with great sadness that we must put to rest our loving Makita, best friend, therapist, love bug, hider of shoes, and guardian. Our beautiful boy was known for his curious ways of greeting the world and his kindness to other living beings. Makita, known as Maki, Muk Muk, and Kee Kee, was a hater of the shower but an avid drinker of bath and toilet water. His best afternoons were spent in the pool and around family BBQs or wrestling with his skin sister. Makita was always there to give comfort during a long spell on the couch or time on the porch.

We will forever remember you in family days by the pool or during Saturday night binge-watching or by the smell of hotdogs cooking. In moments like these, we will remember the Makita dance and zoomies and give thanks for sharing your life.

Preceding departure in death and waiting on Makita at the Rainbow Bridge are his loving Nonna and Grandad. Surviving Makita are his pack mom and dad, his sister Sarah, Grandma, and his lovey, Piggy. In lieu of flowers, you may honor Makita by kissing a dog on the soft spot between his eyes.

13

NOT JUST ANY OLD BALL
By Errol Green, author and animal rescuer

Scooby and his mother were a pair of scrappy survivor Chihuahuas found living on the side of a highway in Carrollton, Georgia, before an organization stepped in to rescue them. When Errol Greene and his wife saw them up for adoption at a local PetSmart in town, he wanted them both. Unfortunately for him, he could only talk his significant other into one, and he took the pup, leaving the founder of the rescue to adopt the pup's mom.

The pup didn't know what was happening but accepted it and slept on Errol's chest all the way home, enjoying his first bath and best meal ever that would be just one of many to come during his years with the Greenes.

Perhaps it was the fact that he'd already lived a tumultuous existence, surviving on dried worms (a delicacy for him he never tired of even after coming home) and whatever vegetation his mom could find for him, but Scooby turned out to be a fearless little fellow. Upon adoption, he immediately bonded with his pack dad and never left his side, whether sleeping or playing, and with his sweet and playful energy, turned out to be the heart and soul of their home.

Errol couldn't have been happier that he'd found such an amazing companion as Scooby, and together, they made an impact wherever they went. Scooby was surprisingly well-behaved and never barked just to bark, nor did he do any of the negative traits that some small dogs are known for. Scooby loved to go riding in the car, feeling the wind rustle through his ears and his head out the window to absorb every magnificent scent as they went.

When they hung out at Lake Lanier, Errol liked to say that Scooby used his superpower of being ridiculously cute to win over other boaters, nearly always managing to snag a treat from everyone he met. He enjoyed life to its fullest and, each morning, wouldn't get out of bed until Errol played at least one game of covers with him. Scooby would roll over on his side and challenge Errol and his wife to put their hands under the blanket, playing a few rounds before he was ready to start his day.

Yes, it is true that Scooby quickly entrenched himself into the deepest recesses of his pack dad's heart, who felt him much more like a son than just a pet. Scooby was his constant companion when he worked late, staying by his side until it was time to retire for the night. After Errol would return from a business trip, Scooby greeted him as though he were the most special human on the face of the earth. He was Errol's animal soul mate and so incredibly special to him.

On the luckiest days—and there were many because he was much too cute to turn down—Errol would take Scooby down to the creek and let him chase the stones he sent skipping across the water. It was Scooby's favorite place in the world, and he loved being allowed to play in the shallow water, usually pining for it throughout the day until he got his way.

Another thing that Scooby loved was his ball. And not just any ball. It was his favorite red squeaky ball.

Errol and his wife named it "Red Ball," and it amused them that Scooby refused to be separated from it for any length of time. One day it was accidentally thrown down their basement stairwell, and before Errol could go after it, Scooby flew through the air and down those stairs, looking like a flying squirrel to rescue it and bring it back up to the light. To say that Scooby obsessed over Red Ball was putting it mildly, and Errol and his wife were careful to make sure nothing ever happened to the ball so that Scooby would always have his most prized possession. By that time, Scooby had a brother who came to join the pack, and though he loved him, he never allowed Joey to touch his beloved Red Ball.

For thirteen wonderful years, Errol had Scooby at his side, being his best friend and making life more wonderful to live just because he was in it. Everything changed, however, when after some suspicious moments, they took Scooby to the veterinarian where he was eventually diagnosed with a brain tumor. They were lucky, though, for after a few rounds of radiation at a local emergency clinic, an MRI showed the tumor was gone.

Ironically, although the tumor was gone, Scooby continued to decline without reason, and doctors couldn't explain why he wasn't improving.

One night, Scooby was extremely restless and just wouldn't stay asleep. After trying everything they could, Errol's wife asked him to settle Scooby downstairs so she could rest for a few hours. Errol took Scooby down and sat with him for some time then set him up in a comfortable place with food and water and returned upstairs to get some sleep himself.

However, the next morning when he came down, he found Scooby in what he could only describe as a catatonic state. Scooby was alive, but he wasn't acting as though he knew what was going on. His eyes darted back and forth without recognition. He didn't seem to smell or know what was going on. Errol and his wife were dumbfounded at the quick downslide and immediately sought medical help.

The news was grim, and the veterinarian said that, along with his other issues, Scooby was too far gone to recover, and in her recommendation, the humane thing was to let him go. Errol was devastated, but he loved Scooby more than himself and would not allow him to suffer. The veterinarian came to their home, and Errol held his dear Scooby until he took his last breath, and his soul left his body.

Thirteen years wasn't enough, and after Scooby's passing, Errol found himself falling into a deep depression. Where was Scooby? What had happened to cause this catatonic state? Was he at peace? Though Errol considered himself a skeptic, he was desperate to know if his best friend was still around him in some way or was just gone forever.

Errol wasn't going to just ask such an important question to anyone. First, he searched the internet and settled on a pet psychic who was supposed to be one of the best. He contacted him, but his hopes were dashed when it took the psychic over twenty guesses to even tell him what breed of dog Scooby was. Errol walked away from the reading, feeling disappointed and taken.

The psychics were giving him—and others who grieved the same way he was for their lost fur children—what they wanted to hear. Move along, folks... Fido is just fine. Pay with credit or cash.

As time went on and Errol lost other animals he loved, he reached out to multiple pet psychics with a message that he was willing to hire them and pay top dollar, but he'd need to know more than these vague generalities. He stated that the most recent dog he lost had very specific circumstances that he wanted verified, and if they could reach her, it would be something she wanted to deliver. Not one psychic was willing to take him up on this offer.

While some of the so-called animal communicators really believed they had the gift, Errol felt some of them lived with themselves by thinking the deception was for the good of the people, to bring them peace. Errol resigned himself to the fact that he'd never know for sure what happened to Scooby and would have to just accept his death and move on.

One evening, a few weeks after Scooby's passing, Errol and his wife were watching television when a woman from Ireland that they had connected with many years before for a totally unrelated reason sent them an email.

"I know this is out of the blue and going to sound very strange, but I was meditating, and your dog came to me. He was standing in shallow water, and his tail was wagging. He looked incredibly happy, and he wants me to let you know he's just fine."

It was the middle of the night, and she said she felt it so strongly that she had to email them right away before she forgot any of the details.

Errol and his wife were floored because this woman could not have known that Scooby absolutely loved playing in shallow water. But what was even more astonishing was one tiny detail she always added.

"He had a red ball in his mouth."

She didn't say he had just any ball.

No, she wrote, "red ball."

Errol was a natural skeptic, so before responding to her, he scoured their social media accounts to see if he'd ever mentioned the red ball or posted a photo of it anywhere. He spent a few days being thorough; though he had his Facebook locked down to private and friends only, he still wanted to make sure.

The red ball was never mentioned or shown in a photo.

Errol knew then that the communication was real. The woman never asked him for money or even claimed she had an ability to speak to animals who had passed on. She only wanted to pass along the message. Errol was glad she did because it gave both of them tremendous peace, and to this day, he considers it the greatest gift he's ever been given.

Errol Greene is an author and animal rescuer based in Johns Creek, GA.

14

---◆---

A MEOW FROM THE HEART

A few years into my biggest mistake—*I mean my first marriage*—I was a completely depressed and sad piece of work. I just couldn't find a way out of my abusive relationship. At only nineteen years old, I worked a full-time job and, at times, added a part-time job in order to pay the bills.

The guy—I can't stand honoring him by calling him a husband—was never one to do drugs or drink, but he was a hit and a miss when it came to keeping a job. He could get one easily because people like him know how to fake a persona and make others think they are pretty cool. However, the facade slides when the guy gets comfortable, and his temper is hard to keep under wraps. There were several times he came home unemployed after having a screaming match at work. Those were always bad evenings because when he wasn't getting his way outside the home, he was even harder to deal with inside the home.

I'll never forget our first place we had together. It was tiny little place that came furnished with an ugly orange chair and green couch. There were even matching green and orange pots and pans in the kitchen left there for us to use. Though it wasn't much, I made it into a cozy little home. My dad bought us a small round glass-top dining table with chairs and a television for the little living room.

The guy hated my dad, and when he went into one of his rages, he picked up the television, yanking the cord out of the wall, then smashed it through the tabletop. He didn't stop there, though.

During that same rage fit—that was triggered because I'd spent time with my own dad—the guy dragged in the hope chest that I received from my parents for my fifteenth birthday. I pleaded with him to stop because that was my only prized possession, but as I stood there sobbing and begging, he climbed on top of it and jumped up and down until the lid was just shards of wood. When he simmered down and took a look at it, he apologized and said it was beyond repair then carried it to the dump.

Those first few years, the guy would break anything and everything he could get his hands on. I eventually took items I wanted to save and hid them in my father's shed.

The guy would later say that he'd been taking steroids during most of our tumultuous time together, but I never saw any. Not only that, but his mother also once told me that he was just like his father who had left them all early on and that she had locked herself in their bathroom many times to escape his father's rage, just as I did her son's.

An unfortunate circumstance of passing down defective genes, I suppose.

We had been married nearly three years when I finally found a new friend to bring me comfort. But surprise— it wasn't a dog! It was a cat. (I slipped that in on you, didn't I?) He was a sleek black boy with tuxedo markings, and we called him Paco. I have no idea how we decided on this name, and I didn't even know what it meant.

Years later, after the incident I'm about to tell you, I discovered that the Native American meaning of *Paco* is "eagle." And the Spanish name means "free." Remember that for the rest of the story.

Paco just arrived one day, like a gift from above. He was really more of a free spirit than a cat—as he would spend time outside as much as he did inside. We didn't even need a litter box, and if we'd had one, he wouldn't have used it. When he needed to go, he went to the door and meowed, looking at us lowly humans with disdain as he waited for us to open it.

Okay, I exaggerate. Paco never looked at me with anything but admiration. I know, weird for a cat, huh? But wow—how I loved that boy. And I needed him so very much at that time.

At first, the guy said there was no way we could have a cat. Absolutely not. But Paco wasn't going anywhere, even if he couldn't come inside, and he finally wore the guy down. (Later he would become a total cat person, which is weird, I know, for an ass like him.)

Paco was finally allowed inside and became a family member.

Would I have rather had a dog than a cat?

No. I would've loved to have a dog, *as well as* Paco. But my life was so unstable at that time, moving place to place and always just barely making rent, that it would've been cruel to force a dog to be a part of it. I wouldn't have been a responsible pet owner that could afford the things a dog needed.

Paco was enough. And just the right companion for what I needed at that time.

It's sad to say, but by then, I had somehow allowed the guy to control every part of my life, which had narrowed to a tiny bubble of going to work and taking care of him. I was no longer allowed to spend time with my parents.

My siblings were off bounds too. Other than when he said so—because he and my twin sister's husband became hunting buddies. When he wanted to hang out with them, we did, but he absolutely didn't want me alone with my twin. Or my little sister.

The guy never acted up in front of my twin's husband because it was then that he played a role of being an okay person. My sister, however, witnessed some of the abuse and even got into an altercation with the guy when he had me down on the floor, taking my weekly paycheck from me. Most of the time, I handed it over without fuss, but I was the one who paid all the bills, and this time, I got resentful at the fact that he didn't contribute nearly as much as I did.

He wrestled me, trying to pull the money out of my pocket, and my sister pulled him off. Things escalated between the two of them with lots of yelling before she walked away. He had the last word, though, because about an hour later, the guy tried to put a cigarette out on her forehead! Needless to say, their future relationship was rocky.

As for my father, he had stepped up and come back to town after he recovered from the aftermath of losing his family to divorce and was very upset that I had married the guy. He had met him that first night when I was fifteen and allowed to go with my sister. Dad knew he was bad news, or at least his gut had told him so.

However, I was married, and he couldn't undo that, but when he found out that the guy was abusing me not only emotionally but physically, he was very upset.

I would not have told my father, but there was an afternoon that the guy and I were in the car, and we were having an argument. I can't remember what it was, but suddenly the guy (who was driving at the time) reached over and grabbed the back of my hair and slammed my face into the dashboard.

Then he did it again.

I was screaming, and I opened the car door and tried to jump out.

The guy kept his right hand tangled in my hair as he drove recklessly and pulled into the empty parking lot of a school.

By a huge coincidence, my dad had been behind us and saw what was happening. He pulled into the lot with us and jumped out of his car then strode over to where the guy was holding my hair and screaming into my face.

When the guy saw my dad, it enraged him, and he jumped out and pulled a knife.

I love my dad and immediately begged the guy to stop and not to hurt him.

Dad was smart. He put his hands up and backed off.

"Let's all calm down and talk this out," he said.

We finally got the guy calmed down, and Dad agreed to meet at our apartment.

Long story short, when the guy and I arrived at the apartment complex, there were police waiting for him. The guy handed me the knife and told me if I knew what was good for me, I wouldn't let them find it.

I was terrified of the guy. And I did what I was told.

They surrounded him, and I was able to slink away with the knife. I ran around the side of the building and saw a mud puddle, where I slid the knife into the very bottom then ran out from the other side of the building.

The authorities never found it, and I refused to press charges. I begged my dad to just let it go, that the guy promised me he was never going to hurt me again.

And he didn't.

Until the next time.

Months later, there was another—as was usual with offenders—abusive incident, and Dad tried to help me again. He rented a house and told no one where it was, then I moved in. The plan was for me to stay with him for free and save my money to pay for a divorce. Well, the guy was stalking me, and one evening, Dad and I had gone to grab a bite to eat. When we returned, we were pulling into the driveway of the rental house, and I saw the guy's car backed in at the back of the house.

I screamed and pointed.

Dad backed out and took off, careening around curves, through stop signs, and driving like a madman because the guy was chasing us and determined to run us down.

It was good thinking on Dad's part because he headed straight for the police station. Unfortunately, it was some distance away, and that meant that Dad had to slide through traffic lights and not stop for anything with the guy still on his tail all the way to the station.

Once in the parking lot, Dad lay on the horn until he got the attention of two police officers who were checking in. By the time they got to our car, the guy was already there, banging on my window and begging me to get out and just let him talk.

I was as far down in the seat as I could possibly get, sure that this was it, and both my dad and I were going to be killed.

Thankfully, they handcuffed the guy and took him into custody.

I was an uncontrollable, shaking mess of fear, and again, I refused to press charges. I'll never forget meeting with the judge who sat with my dad and tried to tell me that I had to make it stop. However, they had never been at the hands of someone who weighed nearly a hundred pounds more than you and could be the taker of your last breath.

I had already seen the guy take on three other young men with a ball bat and nearly beat them to death. Three on one, which resulted in hospital stays.

For them. Not the guy.

Pressing charges would've meant arrest, then bail would be set.

Bail would be paid.

Then he'd find me.

Dad made a deal with the judge. They would keep the guy long enough for my dad to sneak me out of state to a safe and unknown location. But they only gave us twenty-four hours, so we had to move fast.

I didn't want to go. I had been at my job for three years, and it was the only security I knew in life at that time. But honestly, other than that, I had nothing.

So I agreed, and we threw what I could into a car and headed from South Carolina to Kansas, where I moved in with the aunt and uncle I barely knew.

I was a mess. Less than a hundred pounds at that point, I couldn't eat solid food, and my depression was deep. I just could not make myself swallow. Therefore, my aunt would stand over me as I drank the mandated Ensure each day and tried to get down soup.

Then I got a job, and I went back to school.

Briefly.

I was more homesick than I had ever been in my life. And when somehow the guy found out where I was and started calling, he wore me down with promises, and I eventually caved when he promised me a plane ticket home. By then, my car was junk, and I didn't make enough money to purchase a ticket myself. Also, the guy had turned into the crying, begging, I-swear-this-time-I-will-be-good kind of man that I hoped had learned his lesson.

So I went home. On his terms.

And spoiler alert—he hadn't learned his lesson.

That's why my story about Paco is so important.

My dad was disgusted with me that, after all his effort, I went back to the guy. I was disgusted with myself, actually. However, no one else was offering me sanctuary. So I accepted my punishment and went back to having everything I did under the guy's control.

Where I went. What I wore. Who I talked to.

Eventually the guy and I moved out to a place in the country. One particular day, he was in a mood. We argued. Over something stupid, I'm sure.

It escalated.

I tried to leave before it got ugly.

As he'd done a hundred times before, he slung me against a wall and then held me there with his hand against my throat while he expended his rage into my face, screaming and showering me with spittle as he shouted that I wasn't going anywhere.

He was terrifying when he did that, and many times, he held me there until I blacked out. This time I didn't, and when he released me, I sank to the floor but got up and hobbled to the bedroom.

I shut the door, my chest and neck throbbing in pain. *Again.*

I knew I couldn't continue trying to work things out with him. I had to get away.

But how? Once again, he had my car keys and my purse.

For the next twelve to fifteen hours, I lay in there and read books with Paco at my side. Finally, when I peeked out and looked down the hallway, I could see the guy had gone to sleep on the couch.

I thought if I could get out the door, I could go to a neighbor's house and call my dad, and maybe he would come and get me.

Quiet as a mouse, I kissed Paco and promised I'd come back for him then slipped out of the room.

I opened the door very slowly.

I was almost out when it creaked loudly.

Guy was up and off that couch and storming at me a hundred miles an hour, enraged because I dared to try to leave.

Filled with sudden terror, I made a dash for it and was quickly off the porch and running up the gravel driveway, panicked as he gained ground.

The guy finally lunged and grabbed my hair from behind and jerked me backward. I caught my fall with my hands, but they were instantly bloodied from the gravel, and my knees followed suit as the guy started dragging me back to the house.

We struggled up the steps, and inside, he slung me back into the small dark bedroom and slammed the door. I was hurt bad on the outside. And on the inside, I was completely broken. But you know what I had?

Paco.

My beloved cat stayed with me every minute, and to this very day, I remember how sad he looked when he licked at the tears that ran down my face and listened to my sobs.

I eventually forgave the guy again. What choice did I have?

At the time, no one ever told me there was any such thing as women's shelters. I had no idea. All I knew was that my family couldn't give me refuge, and though the guy didn't work all the time, somehow, he contributed enough to help me keep a roof over our heads.

But I couldn't do it alone. Or at least I thought I couldn't.

Admittedly, I was also young and full of hope that one day he would be different. He could be very nice when he wanted to, and he could talk a good game about the future we could have.

After each incident, he would usually be good to me for a few weeks or months, making me feel that maybe what we had would work. He also made me believe that I was ugly and was lucky that he had chosen me and that no one else would ever want me.

It wasn't hard to believe when your world consisted of not much else other than a man who sometimes claimed to love you while other times was slamming you into the wall and choking you out.

Four years into the marriage, I got pregnant with my first daughter. That would change the guy for sure, I thought. And it did. But only for a while.

There were still rages.

Even an incident of him pulling me down a flight of stairs by my hair then kicking me in my swollen stomach. I thought a child would change him, but all me being pregnant did was make him even more possessive and jealous. More controlling. He even timed me when I went to the grocery store, screaming at me and accusing me of cheating if I were even a few minutes late.

Life was not fun.

Nor healthy.

I was relieved to have Paco. My only friend.

Eight months into my pregnancy, a hurricane came raging across the east coast with such an impact that it reached as far inland as we lived. In the middle of the night, very close to my due date, we left to evacuate to a safer place.

In the chaos, Paco slipped out the door and was gone in a frightened flash.

There was no time to waste, and we left, me sobbing in worry about my sweet boy. As the storm raged that night, I prayed for God to protect Paco and give him sanctuary. I prayed that he would make it through the storm and that, most of all, he wouldn't be frightened.

It was a very long night.

When we returned the next day, making our way around fallen trees, power lines, and more aftermath, Paco was nowhere to be found.

Spending the first night in that house where I lived most of my time in the small dark bedroom was devastating without Paco beside me. Using money I couldn't afford for print fees and gas for my car, I made up flyers and went door to door for miles outside the parameter of our home, asking if anyone had seen him.

I prayed harder than I'd ever prayed, begging for God to send him back to me.

Paco never returned.

It was as though he'd disappeared off the face of the earth.

Remember how I told you that his name also means *eagle*?

Had he flown away from the hurricane? To somewhere safe?

To this day, I thank God that I had Paco for the period that I did, for his comfort meant the world to me at a time when I had no one else. I still hold the hope that he was needed in another worse situation than mine as that is the only way I can live with the guilt that I left him to face the storm alone. Or could it be that God let him be mine for the time I needed, and Paco was only passing through?

Psalm 55:6–8: "And I say, 'If only I had wings like a dove, I would fly away and be at rest. Yes, I would go far away. I would live in the desert. I would hurry to my safe place, away from the wild wind and storm.'"

15

IN LOVING MEMORY OF PACO

We lay to rest the fondest memories of Paco, the swashbuckling tuxedo cat, who disappeared in the aftermath of Hurricane Hugo.

Paco was a cat who appreciated his freedom, splitting his time between his outdoor hunting expeditions and his indoor therapy sessions, specializing in counseling and compassion as it related to domestic abuse. Paco was known as one of the best cats who knew his way around a face of tears.

In Paco's honor, we would like to take this opportunity to announce that not every human is made to be a lover of dogs, and that being a cat person or a crazy cat lady is also just fine with the universe.

Paco was dearly missed by the troubled young woman he guarded and has made a silent promise to one day haunt the unpredictable guy who made her life a living hell, who, in another twist of fate, later became a cat person.

In honor of Paco, the therapy cat who enjoyed his freedom too much for one last time, please sniff some catnip and try to climb the nearest tree, just not in the middle of a hurricane.

16

———◆———

A HAPPY ROLO CAMPER
By Jordan, retired Police Chief and veteran

I want to start this story out with the claim that I have the utmost respect for the law and what those in blue do to protect and serve. That's why when I read this account and saw that it was written by a retired police chief with twenty-five years of service, as well as eight years in the army, it piqued my interest. I don't know many past law enforcement or veterans who would jeopardize their reputation with a fabricated tale.

I'll call this man Jordan, and his story, as it relates to our subject about *do dogs have souls or spirits,* is about his little buddy, Rolo.

Rolo came to them through an organization that rescued him from an abusive home. After all that the tiny terrier had been through, he didn't trust easy and was quite jumpy, but once he sensed that he was safe with Jordan, he became his shadow and protector.

Once secure in his new role, Rolo took his position seriously and was completely devoted to the family but especially to Jordan, who he knew had saved him and given him a safe place to call home. With a new sense of security and routine, Rolo learned to love life again.

Some of the little dog's favorite times were when he

accompanied the family on their camping trips. Not only did Rolo get to adventure out and see new places, smell fresh scents, and get treats like grilled hot dogs and patties, but he was praised often for his guarding skills when a stranger or a random critter would happen upon them.

Jordan and his family learned that being a part of a happily-ever-after story for a living creature who possibly thought it would never happen for him was one of the biggest blessings you could be given. They loved Rolo deeply. And he returned that love fully for nearly twenty long years.

It was a very bittersweet decision two years after Rolo died to finally take another camping trip without the one who loved it the most.

However, Jordan was busy one afternoon getting supplies ready for the trip when, out of the corner of his eye, Rolo sauntered into the garage and circled three times as he had always done then plopped down to take a nap at Jordan's feet.

Jordan knew he wasn't seeing things, but he stayed calm and didn't say a word because he didn't want to alarm his family.

A few hours later, he'd nearly forgotten about his experience when he heard a scream from the kitchen. He and his wife both ran in to find their daughter standing in front of the refrigerator where she'd been pulling out chicken to pack in the ice cooler for the weekend.

"It was Rolo," she exclaimed. "He just came running in and begged for a piece of chicken and then faded away! I swear it. I saw him plain as day."

Jordan knew he had to share what he'd seen earlier, and as a family, they talked about what a wonderful gift they'd been given, but his wife was a bit disappointed that she had not been witness to it.

Rolo must've heard her because they headed out the

next morning, and after they'd arrived at the camping ground and set up, she was alone in the camper and looked up to see him lying on the couch, curled up and asleep.

When she blinked and looked again, he was gone.

He didn't show himself anymore after those events, but the family was at peace knowing that little Rolo was still with them, all around them, and accompanying them on his favorite adventures until, once again, they will be reunited in another realm.

17

BE NOT AFRAID

Three years after my first daughter, Heather Nicole, was born, I had finally had enough. Do you want to know what tipped the scale? It had nothing to do with how many times he had hurt me, shoving me and choking me, or having total control over me.

It was the night that the guy came in from playing basketball all day at the local recreation center and pitched one of his rages because I had cooked spaghetti for supper.

He didn't like spaghetti.

But that was all I had, and our toddler liked it, so that was what I went with.

The guy cussed me out and then went through the living room where Heather was sitting at her children's table in front of the television, eating her spaghetti. He kicked the table right out from under her, sending it and all the food flying into the air and her scrambling into my arms.

That was the first time he'd ever crossed the line with her, but in an instant, I saw our life through her eyes, that of a child who didn't know why her father was red and screaming like a madman. Heather was my child, the one I prayed for and received, the one I thanked God for every hair on her little head and promised to love and protect her.

That was it. No more faltering. No more weak spine.

I didn't cuss back. I didn't do anything except comfort my daughter and quietly clean the mess up—or as much as I could considering it was red sauce on white carpet. By then, I had no more fight in me, even if I had wanted to argue back.

When I had everything cleaned up, I waited until he was in the shower, and I took Heather, and we left. I didn't have anywhere to go because I didn't want to bring trouble to anyone I loved, so we just drove around. Soon I found myself passing a church and could see people filing in for the evening service.

I don't know what got into me, because I hadn't been in church for years, but like a moth to the flame, I pulled in. My daughter and I went in, avoiding eye contact or shaking hands with anyone. I was too vulnerable and emotional to make nice.

When the music segment began and people started singing, I could feel my nerves start to settle. Then when the organ began the song "I Surrender All," the tears came. I felt so alone, so broken and afraid. I asked God to be with me and give me strength.

I knew I was going to be in danger by leaving because, if he couldn't talk his way back, he would find me and drag me back. I had tried to leave him the year before. I took Heather and went out to my mom's house. She didn't have room for me there, but as I was trying to figure out what to do, he came flying up the road and into the driveway.

He told me to get my ass into the truck.

I declined.

He knew how to manipulate me. He strode right past me, into the house, and picked up our daughter then went back out the door.

Outside, I tried to get her back from him. He pushed me away and went to the truck and threw her into the front seat. I was trying to get the door open on the other side, and he came around and reared back and slapped me so hard that I flew across the hood of his truck and catapulted into the gravel driveway.

Then he got into the truck and peeled gravel, taking off at a high speed.

With my baby crying and without a safety seat.

I desperately tried to call him. He wouldn't answer. Finally, I got in touch with his mother, who confirmed that he'd deposited our baby with her, and she was fine.

He didn't want her. He only wanted to hurt me.

I went back. I couldn't chance him taking her away from me.

But that day when he exploded again in front of her, something clicked.

A week from that day, I sat in front of a lawyer and spilled out my story through a mess of tears and wracking sobs. I had never told anyone every detail, and the purging of it was like a raging, out-of-control fire that had to burn down. I told him about the day the guy locked me in an empty room for sixteen hours while he and his friends played cards right outside. And the morning he took me out to the woods and carried a gun that he planned to kill me with, and I made him believe I wasn't going to leave to get out of dying. And all the times he'd ripped my uniforms to shreds because he thought I was talking to another guy at work, and he didn't want me to go. And kicked me when I was pregnant, went out with his friends, and left me home.

And the emotionally devastating time he brought another woman to my bed when I was away. (I found where she'd left her phone number and called her. She told me everything, and that was the only time that I laid my hands on him. He came in the door that night, and

I kept punching his chest. He stood there and let me, crying and begging for forgiveness.)

And the afternoon he found a sock of quarters in my underwear drawer and was so enraged at me for "hiding money" that he stomped over to his mother's house where I was visiting, yanked me out of there, and dragged me across the street to our home then beat me up.

Then there was the time he did something so heinous to me that I cannot even bear to write it in this book, and the memory makes me sick to my stomach. Something that could send him straight to hell if he doesn't ask God for forgiveness. Something that showed how dark and evil he truly is inside.

I laid it all out there for the attorney. I'm not an overly dramatic person. I don't laugh a lot, and I don't cry a lot. I'm introspective and practical when I speak. Logical and a realist. I am sensitive, and I'll admit that. But I'm like a soldier in the face of pain.

That lawyer believed every word I said. Then he had mercy and worked out a payment plan for me, and I put on my big-girl panties and went home and told the guy that I meant it this time.

I told him in a public place, and though I acted stronger than I ever had before, I was scared. I did good because this time, there was something that made him believe me. Miraculously, he moved out. I had to give him every penny I had to make him do it, but it was worth being broke.

We started the one-year separation.

I'd love to say it was easy from then on out, but it wasn't. The guy went back and forth between hating me and wanting me back. He stalked me, even going as far as terrorizing me one night when I was in my new apartment alone and breaking my door down as the police came racing up just in time.

That door had two dead bolts and a knob lock on it, yet he kicked it completely out of the doorframe, causing a very expensive number of damages. He showed superhero strength in his rage, fueled by his paranoia that I had someone else in there with me.

I did not. And I *was not* dating anyone at that time.

I was much too scared for that.

In his self-defense, for some of the later incidents in our marriage, he tried to tell people that I had an affair during our last year together. The truth is this, I did indeed have a manager (he was single) that was a sounding board to me for a long time. In that last year, we got too close. I'll admit that, but remember, during this time, I was barely allowed to be around my family, and I had no friends at all. I'm not excusing anything, and I don't condone my actions. I'm just telling how a young woman can fall into that kind of thing.

At work, talking to my manager, I felt he cared about me and what was happening.

For two years or more, it was simply a harmless friendship, but then, during one of my many separations from the guy in that last year, I had a weak moment and was lonely.

My friend (and manager) urged me to meet him outside of work. He wasn't going to take no for an answer, and he continued to badger me, which I now know was completely inappropriate in the workplace and just in general, considering how vulnerable I was. He argued that the guy and I were not living under the same roof, and the guy was out seeing other women, so why shouldn't I see other men?

I gave in, and we saw each other a handful of times, and it was no longer innocent.

To this day, I regret it and feel I only did it out of a deep sense of loneliness and as revenge for what the guy did when he brought a woman to our home. It was strange that his indiscretion hurt me emotionally, much more than his hands ever did physically.

Looking back, I should've waited to see anyone else on a personal level until I was divorced. And after the very brief thing—fling?—when the guy and I got back together, it was done. From then on, we were only friends, and even that ended when he got married and was transferred to another place of employment.

I told the attorney about that regret.

The only other confession I had was that *after* the abusive moments, I would "talk back," as the guy called it.

"Don't talk back to me!" he'd scream in my face as he shoved me against the wall.

"Oh, does that make you feel like a real man?" One of my common retorts.

I never *caused* him to erupt. He did that on his own for the most stupid and unworthy things. But after—once I was trying to recover from the attack—I'd tell him only weak men hurt women. And yes, I called him names.

Even if they were whispered at him while he stomped away.

I couldn't hurt him back physically, but I was not going to keep my mouth shut after he put his hands on me and caused me pain. Was it wrong for me to say things back? Maybe. It earned me a lot more pain too. But sometimes my only defense was letting him know what kind of man I thought he was. Anyone who knows me in my life since then and now knows I'm not that person. I'm not the type of girlfriend or wife you see on reality shows, flinging insults.

I wasn't then, and I'm not now.

Believe what you will. There is never any excuse to lay your hands on another human being in anger. Nothing will ever justify the abuse he inflicted on me.

I wish the young girl that was me knew that truth back then.

More months followed with calls telling me he was going to blow his brains out if I didn't come back, as well as more harassment at my job. By then, I was working at the Cracker Barrel part time, in addition to my full-time job. After a few times that I had to be escorted safely to my car because of the guy, the manager told me that it was best if I came back after the divorce and things had calmed down.

If you are wondering about a restraining order, or what some call a protective order, yes—been there and done that. To the guy, it was a worthless piece of paper and didn't serve any purpose in telling him what he could and couldn't do with *his* wife.

The months dragged on, and I prayed continuously for safety and courage.

Finally, the court date arrived, and with my dad by my side as support, I walked in.

When they called my name, I was ushered in to stand before the judge. I was so terrified that I was trembling, even my teeth chattering so hard I could barely speak. My body was wracked with pain from the quaking and the nerves.

Luckily, the guy didn't show up.

The judge read through all the documents and reports of harassment, and then he looked up at me. "Young lady, I hope you see that this is a new lease on life for you," he said then went into cases he'd seen that had ended in tragedy and stressed my need to once and for all end things.

I nodded, unable to speak.

He signed the papers and granted my divorce on the grounds of physical abuse.

The guy didn't show up.

I'd love to say that walking out of that courthouse, I felt a new sense of freedom, and I suppose in a way, I did. Unfortunately, I would always have a physical reminder of my tumultuous seven years with a lifelong issue in my neck with a bad disk and a routine slice of agony through my chest at random times that feels like having a heart attack.

After many tests over several years, the doctor said I would carry the aftereffects from a chest-wall injury—and neck pain with me always—the collateral damage of being thrown against the wall and held there by my neck so many times.

Many years later, just before a doctor diagnosed me with Fibromyalgia, he would ask me if I'd ever gone through periods of physical or emotional pain that could've triggered the syndrome.

By then, I was too proud and ashamed to tell anyone of my past.

Even if I didn't have those burdens, life wasn't easy by any means for a young single mother. I had a full-time job with benefits, but it didn't pay enough to cover my bills. That meant I had to get a second job, which I did, slinging sausage patties at the crack of dawn in a country gas station for all the early bird workers who stopped in for biscuits.

Then I had the complication of finding childcare that didn't cost more than I made.

Before the divorce, my daughter's paternal grand-mother used to keep her granddaughter for free, but afterwards, she decided she needed to be paid, even knowing that I barely had two pennies to rub together.

Somehow, though, I was pulling it all together at the last moments.

We were surviving.

When my sister found a nice place in the country for me, I proudly decorated it with the stuff I had and felt a sense of accomplishment at having my first home com-pletely on my own.

That ended within a few months when the owner of

the place, a man at least thirty years my senior, cornered me when I went to pay the rent. He tried to kiss me, scaring me to death, and said we could make an arrangement if I needed a break on the rent.

I pushed him off me and fled. I was terrified to stay in my home because he had keys to my doors. I didn't have anyone to call for help, so dreading when dark came and I'd be at the mercy of the old pervert, I reluctantly knocked at a neighbor's house.

He listened to my story then went out and bought dead bolts and installed them for me. I still locked my daughter and me in the bedroom at night, terrified that the landlord would find a way in.

We struggled, but my daughter never knew it. She was just a toddler, and I shielded her from my worries. I was still dealing with her dad—the guy—and on the days that my daughter wasn't with me, I was afraid to be home alone. I spent a lot of time (when I wasn't working) at the nearby graveyard. No one had a clue about finding me there, and I could read and nap, feeling secure among people who meant me no harm.

Several months after my divorce, I started dating a young man I'll call Garfield. He was a really nice person. Had a great job. Nice family. Money saved and plans to build a home of his own soon. He was a handsome fellow, and he really liked me. The icing on the cake was that my daughter was fond of him too. Garfield made it clear that he wanted to make my life easier, and I appreciated him for that. I liked him a lot.

But I could not see myself in love with him.

I had already married before out of desperation, and no matter how hard life was, I wasn't going to do it again. When I discovered he planned to give me a ring for Christmas, I broke up with him. He was upset, and I felt so guilty.

But not guilty enough to give him the rest of my life.

I dated a few others but found out really quick that being a single mother, with my first priority being a toddler and the second one my work responsibilities, didn't make me a prime pick for eligible bachelors that weren't creeps. The few that I had some dates with were only interested in instant gratification, not in a real relationship.

One man who I thought could turn out to be a possible candidate told me that I was too good for a scoundrel like him. I felt rejected, but turns out, he was right.

I was better off alone.

18

BELLE AND THE BRIDGE
By Suzette, wife, mother, and retired real estate agent

In my research for this book, I ran across a story that a woman named Suzette, a wife, mother, and retired real estate agent, posted about her dog, Belle. She wrote it from her heart, and I could feel her emotion pouring out of the words I read.

I contacted her, and we chatted back and forth.

After talking to her, I felt confident enough in her background and what she knows as her truth to share her words in this book, as follows.

One week ago, we made the heartbreaking decision to send our beloved Belle to Heaven. We knew my mom would be waiting for her at the other side of the Rainbow Bridge.

When we arrived back home in silence and got out of the car, a small voice spoke to my heart, whispering, "Look to the East." Knowing Jerusalem is located to the east, I wanted to see what splendor God must have in store for us.

At the moment, we turned the corner to our house, and there, in all of its glorious color, was a rainbow starting to form! I sobbed tears of joy, realizing God was letting us know we had made the right decision at the right time.

A sprinkling of rain came down and blessed us as we stood in amazement, looking at the rainbow. I took hundreds of photographs with my cell phone because I could not believe the miracle I was witnessing of God's love for us.

And then the second miracle started to form... the silhouette of Belle's beautiful face. The face of a springer spaniel has distinct markings, and those markings appeared just above the rainbow.

As each moment passed, the face became more apparent. It was her exact markings of color that were characteristic to Belle's face alone. I took more photos and cried more tears of joy that we were witnessing the actual Rainbow Bridge our beloved animals cross over to get into Heaven.

It was real, and it was tangible.

To know and trust in one's heart what God has promised us is one thing, but to witness it in person is another level of trust and joy. God was with us and wanted us to know, without a doubt, that Belle was on her way to Heaven via the Rainbow Bridge.

God allowed the bridge to stay within our view for over an hour.

I could not walk away until I saw the bridge become smaller and smaller until it harmoniously blended with the magnificent storm clouds surrounding us.

God gave His grace abundantly to us that night so we may never have thoughts of doubt... His promises are true. We will see our beloved animals again in Heaven one day.

Thank you, God, for entrusting us with Belle for thirteen years. But even more importantly is that God entrusted us with the vision of His Rainbow to ensure we would tell our family and friends of the promises He will always keep.

God is the same yesterday, today, and tomorrow.

There *is* a Heaven, and there is definitely a Rainbow Bridge!

Jesus, I Trust in You.

*In some history reports, the origin of the famed Rainbow Bridge comes from the Norse legend of the Bifröst in which the bridge connects the world of the gods to the one of humanity and is lush with green meadows and hills for all our departed dogs to roam and play until they are reunited with us.

"[God] comforts us in all our troubles so that we can comfort others. When they are troubled, we will be able to give them the same comfort God has given us" (2 Corinthians 1:4 NLT).

19

YOUR LOVE AMAZES ME

When my twenty-fourth birthday rolled around, I was finally forced to allow my daughter to go with her dad for a weekend. To say it put me into a deep dark place is putting it mildly. I worked my Saturday job and then went home and straight to bed.

It was my birthday, but I didn't care.

However, my mom did. She wasn't a drinker, but she liked to go to the local boot-scootin' country place to listen to music. That evening, she stormed my bedroom and told me to get my lazy butt out of bed and go with her.

I declined.

She insisted.

I didn't want to go. I really didn't. I think I was feeling quite sorry for myself and wanted to wallow in my pity party while I didn't have to hide it from my daughter. However, my mom wasn't going to let me stay there all alone on my birthday, so we negotiated an hour.

My plan was to get in, do my hour, then get home and go to bed early.

God had other plans.

I didn't go to bars. I didn't drink either. I had no idea what to order, but I wanted to look like I knew what I was doing. Beer smelled terrible to me, and the only drink I'd ever heard of was called Sex on the Beach, so that was what I ordered.

When I got it, from what I remember, it was sickly sweet, but I sipped on it as we listened to the band. A few men came and asked me to dance, but I declined.

At that time, I'd been told many times that I was ugly and no one would ever want me. I was surprised to get asked, but I couldn't accept. I had never danced with a man before and didn't have a clue how to do it.

Just before the hour was over, my mom whispered to me that there was a guy over yonder who hadn't taken his eyes off me since he'd walked in.

I looked and saw a tall, handsome fellow leaning against a pole, his eyes on me.

In his cowboy boots and jeans, tall and lanky, with muscles and a chiseled face, he was much too handsome to be attracted to me.

I looked away immediately and told my mom that he must be looking at someone behind us.

"I'm going to go order another Coke, and we'll see if he comes over while I'm gone," she said. I tried to grab her back. I didn't want the test. But she was up and gone.

She was right.

He approached slowly. I could feel my heart thudding in my chest.

"I have to tell you that you have the prettiest blue eyes I've ever seen."

Oh Lordy—how cheesy.

But the smile that went with the line was genuine and kind. And so damn sexy.

I wasn't expecting that. His compliment left me tongue-tied, and I laughed nervously.

He asked me to dance—the part I was dreading.

I shook my head, telling him I didn't know how, but

he reached for my hand and pulled me to my feet and to the dance floor.

The band was on break, and a song called "Your Love Amazes Me" by John Berry was playing. Romeo told me his name and apologized for being stiff, stating that he was in town for a softball circuit and was sore. His cousins had talked him into stopping by the little hole-in-the-wall called Possum Holler on the way home.

He was indeed moving a little stiffly, which made my inept and graceless dancing appear to be halfway decent. I really appreciated that he didn't hold me too close like I'd seen other men doing to the women on the dance floor. Instead, he danced with me like he thought I was proper, as they say in the south.

He was right. As far as a divorced young mother goes and despite the things that I'd been through, I was proper. Very much more so than the average young adult of my age. I wasn't innocent, by any means, but I wasn't some girl out to find a guy to bring home.

I know it sounds made-up, but there were sparks. I had never had sparks with anyone before, so the giddy feeling, sweating palms, and racing pulse were all new to me.

After the dance, he told me his name, but his southern accent was so strong and the music was so loud, I didn't catch the last part. I only knew his first name was Ben.

I told him my name, and he asked if he could have my number. I scrawled it down on a napkin—just like in the movies!—and gave it to him. When I returned to the table with my mom, of course I got a bunch of I-told-you-so comments, but she could see that I was beaming.

Soon after that dance—the only one I accepted the few hours I stayed—I went home. This was in the days before cell phones, so every day when I got off work that next week, I raced to get my daughter and get home in case Mister-Tall-Blonde-and-Handsome-Ben-With-

No-Last-Name called me. I left my part-time job, and for three weeks, I did the same thing, feeling more discouraged each day.

I had thought he really liked me, and his silence reinforced my lifelong struggle with the complex that I wasn't worthy. I finally gave up, telling myself that he found someone prettier than I was, probably someone who wasn't a single mother, scraping by to make ends meet. Someone with a better future than me.

At that time, I was in my sixth year working retail management for the same company. Even as a manager, the pay was still not enough to do more than barely get by. Since I had left my part-time job and my daughter's birthday was coming up, I asked the owner of the Holler if I could waitress on the weekends that I didn't have Heather at home.

I had never waited tables or worked in a bar, but I only wanted to work long enough to save enough tips to buy Heather a swing set for her upcoming birthday. I was hired.

On the second weekend of that gig, Ben came back in.

The place had a second-floor area. I had just gone up to take orders and was coming back down the stairs with a tray in my hand and a towel over my arm when I met him coming up.

We both stopped as we met. It was really awkward. I wanted to just walk by him like I didn't remember his face, but I couldn't. No matter how weird it felt, I had to know.

"You never called me," I said.

"You gave me the wrong number."

I looked at him with doubt. Was he playing me?

He pulled the piece of paper out and showed it to me.

He was right. My number had been changed multiple times because every time the guy would get it and start hounding me, I'd change it again. I suppose that night, in my nervousness of meeting Ben, I had transposed the numbers.

He thought I had done it on purpose, and I thought he just didn't want to talk to me. However, he said he had to know why I gave him the wrong number because he'd felt a spark too. He came back to see if he could find me. We both realized that it was a miscommunication, and he asked me out on a date for the next weekend.

Barely able to believe my luck, I accepted, and the next weekend, I met him at a restaurant. I wasn't about to let a stranger come to my home where I was raising my young daughter, so I wanted to check him out in public first. That night, we ate and then drove around and talked for hours and hours.

Ben lived an hour away and worked a lot of hours, but every minute that he could, he would call and talk to me. Over the next few weeks, he would come to see me on the weekends, and because I had a young daughter there, he would stay at the local motel. I quit the bar job when I got enough tips to buy that swing set, and Ben came over and put it together for me. Then he changed the oil in my car. I think he even went around and fixed some things in my house that had been bugging me since moving in.

Other than my dad, I had never been around a guy—well, a man—who knew how to do stuff and do it effortlessly. I had also never had someone want to take care of me.

I was enthralled. I found out that day that he was eight years older than me, but being the old soul I've always been, we didn't feel any distance in age.

Ben loved that at the source of my heart, I just wanted a simple life full of kindness, and I loved that he had grown up with a foundation of believing in God, with a solid and supportive family, and was just an overall good person.

Three weeks after our first date, we wished so badly that we lived closer to one another so we could spend more time together.

On that Friday preceding Memorial Day, Ben came to visit again. My daughter was gone to her dad's, so I said he could sleep on the couch. I know right here you are thinking that I'm full of bologna, that Ben and I had plans to do the funky monkey. I don't care what you believe, but I'm telling you, it wasn't so. I was a good girl, and though I was head over heels, I didn't know if he felt it as much as I did.

However, I wasn't totally naïve. I made a huge dinner of home-cooked food, because you know what they say, a way to a man's heart is through his stomach, and I was after that heart.

Ben was a big eater, and I loved to cook. When I proudly set out the fried chicken, mashed potatoes and gravy, and corn on the cob—that, by the way, was an expensive dinner for me to create—he declined, stating he wasn't hungry.

This was a man who absolutely loved to eat.

I was instantly worried.

He was going to break up with me. I just knew it.

Instead, he took a seat against the wall on the floor and looked up at me.

"Would you think about marrying me one day?"

My heart soared, and I was ecstatic that he was not breaking up with me. I immediately said yes, I would. I couldn't contain the smile that stretched across my face.

Someone wanted me. Not just any someone either. A good someone!

"What day?" he said next.

I laughed, and he jumped up and hugged me, and from that evening on, we started making plans to merge our lives together. He admitted that he'd sunk to the floor because he was so nervous that I'd say no, he felt faint.

That night, after we both went to bed, I sneaked into the living room and smiled as I saw his six-foot-three lanky body squished up on my couch, his feet hanging over the end.

He looked so uncomfortable that I woke him.

"You can sleep in my bed, Ben, but you have to stay on your side."

Immediately, he agreed. He was exhausted from a long workweek, and the couch just wasn't getting it.

We started out on our own sides of the bed, but then he jumped on me like a madman.

Okay, full disclosure. He was a perfect gentleman, but I couldn't sleep with that big hunk of handsome man within inches of me.

I made the first move.

That was all he needed to know.

We were in love.

So, so much in love that we were like giddy, giggling teenagers.

Ben made me feel like I'd won the lottery by him finding me—and my daughter. I knew I had hit the big time. Here was a good-looking man from a good family with a great job and a future! And he said he loved me.

Originally, we started sketching out details for a small wedding. It was going to be a very informal event with just a few family members. Unfortunately, after I booked chairs and a few other rental items, I started to get more harassment from the guy.

On the fifth week that Ben and I were dating, my daughter went to her dad's, and Ben took me on an impromptu day trip to the mountains.

We drove into Cocke County, Tennessee and landed in Newport, a tiny town of about seven thousand residents. We weren't there for a tour or a history lesson, though interestingly enough, with so many remote Appalachian hollows for hiding the illegal stills along with the thick forest areas all around, Cocke County was once notorious as a moonshine hot spot. There was a maze of networking set up to move the illegal liquor from the sticks of Cocke County to the busy towns and cities and into the hands of those who were eager to partake, as they once called it. Extortion and bribery were also rampant within law-enforcement circles to keep the endeavors going from the roaring twenties to at least 1960.

A captivating scenario, but I didn't know any of that back then. I was only interested in the young man driving my car and stealing my heart.

Ben turned to look at me. "You know we could get married today right here. There's no waiting period in Cocke County."

"Sounds good to me," I said, thinking he was kidding.

When he drove straight to their county courthouse, I realized he was serious.

It was a grand but imposing building, built in 1930 after the original structure that was built in 1886 burnt to the ground. By the time we got out of our car, the storm had arrived and we ran through the pouring rain into the building and found the appropriate office. We told the girl at the desk that we wanted to get married right then.

She laughed and told us that it was a slight problem because the judge that did the marrying there was actually working part time over at the hardware store. She could do the paperwork, but we would need to go get the judge to finish the ceremony.

I froze.

It wasn't that I didn't want to really marry him. I had one little problem. Remember when I said I didn't catch his last name that first night? Well, I still didn't know it. I never wanted to admit that I hadn't understood him. Then as time passed, I was too embarrassed to ask. This was before social media, and there was no opportunity for me to sleuth it out!

However, I realized I could just linger and let him pull out his identification first and catch a peek.

I couldn't catch the peek. But as it was time to sign the papers, I slid them over and told Ben to go first and then got a look at what my new last name was about to be.

Thankfully, I liked it!

Have you ever heard that song by Carrie Underwood called "And I Don't Even Know My Last Name"? That should've been our song. Each time I hear it, I'm taken back to that moment and still can't believe that practical, levelheaded me threw caution to the wind and not only married someone I'd only known for eight weeks and only dated for five of those, but signed papers to marry someone when I didn't even know his last name!

My twin sister would later tell me I'd lost my mind.

Back to the car we ran then headed over to the hardware store in the quaint little downtown. Inside, a woman asked if I needed assistance, and I was too shy to say what I was looking for, so I answered I was just browsing.

I made Ben do the asking. He was told we were at the wrong hardware store, and the judge worked at the other one.

Back out into the rain we went, on to the other store.

In there we were told the judge had just left to go fishing.

Can you believe our luck? This is one hundred percent exactly how the day unfolded, and no, we weren't stuck in a Mayberry sitcom.

Ben was not to give up easily. Still happy and hopeful, we headed back to the courthouse and to the same girl who had sent us over to the hardware store. When we told her our problem, she gave us a long look then said she was going to make it happen. She probably thought

I was pregnant, but I wasn't.

"Follow me," she said, leading us through the back hallways. "There's another judge who was going to leave early for the holiday weekend. He might still be here."

That judge was there but packing up his things.

Our clerk explained that we really, really wanted to be married. At first, the judge wasn't happy to have his early exit cut off, but seeing something in the way that we waited for his answer, he got cheerful and prepared to marry us.

A security guard was whistling as he walked down the hall, catching the judge's attention. He called him in to be our witness. Then, a few words and five minutes later, we were married.

We were ecstatic and wanted to shout it out to the world. Once outside the courthouse, Ben insisted we needed rings. At that time, both of us pinched every penny to make ends meet, so by the time we pooled what we had together, it was less than three hundred dollars to our name.

We took two hundred of it and stopped at a jewelry store, buying the cheapest set they offered, which was thankfully on sale for less than three hundred dollars.

Ben found out that most of his family was together at the beach, so using the rest of our pooled money, we drove the few hours back to my town and picked up my daughter then drove four hours to the beach.

When we arrived, it was late, and Ben's mother, a sweet little old-fashioned southern lady, fluttered around us, making a fuss. It was a houseful there with Ben's sister's family and his parents. I had met them once, and I was a bit shy, but my cheeks were about to get hotter.

"I've made a bed up for you and Heather down the hall," his mom said to me. "It's tiny, but you should be fine."

She turned to Ben. "Benjie, you'll have to sleep in the van."

Ben shook his head, declining the invitation to sleep alone. "Nope, I can sleep with them, and we don't care how small it is. We're married, Mama," he said.

That got everyone's attention, and the room quieted.

"Oh, Benjie." His mom laughed, swatting at him. "Stop it. You are sleeping in that van."

She wasn't about to have any before-marriage non-sense happening under her roof, even if it would be a slim chance with a toddler in the bed.

Ben pulled out our marriage certificate and flashed it around.

It took us a few minutes, but we convinced them that yes, we'd eloped. That night in the tiny room, in the smallest bed of a modest beach house, we slept bliss-fully together, as a family.

But would our spur-of-the-moment union and happily ever after last? With the luck I'd had so far in life, I was afraid to hope.

20

FINDING FOREVER & FUREVER

Ben and I started our life together so very modestly, building the foundation of our marriage one brick at a time to keep it sturdy and strong. Just over a year after we'd run through the rain, chasing down the judge in Cocke County, we were blessed to have a daughter together.

Our Amanda Michelle.

I was happy.

So, so happy.

My husband was my best friend, and I finally felt safe.

Then, after years of working retail with low pay and then two years of owning my own housekeeping business that I had to give up because of my neck and back pain, I got the courage to apply for my first office job. I laugh now because I faked my way through the interview, and when they hired me to input orders for purchase agreements, I kept losing my Excel document.

I'd call the tech guy, and he would come down.

"It just keeps disappearing," I told him, bewildered.

He would find it then leave me for a while, and it would happen again.

What I didn't know was that he was having fun with my ignorance and lack of computer skills. I had no idea that I was minimizing the document, and it was still there at the bottom of my screen. That was how little I knew about computers.

But I learned fast.

Super fast.

For a high school dropout who only had a GED, I was earning a lot of brownie points with management for my work ethic, attitude, and ability to figure things out.

I was also really good at organization and multitasking.

I grew confident and went to the university to attend classes in their human resources certification. I had forgotten how much I loved to learn. Even though leaving the girls at night was hard for me, those months were some of my best because I was back in a classroom situation and feeding my brain. I also had a knack for learning the legal human resources details. My favorite was case law, and I devoured the stories of employees and companies in litigation, and I was able to easily memorize law and regulations.

By then, I was working in human resources, and I was promoted to a position as Human Resources Assistant to the Vice President of HR. Amusingly, he would later tell me that I was the best assistant he had ever had but was never going to get anywhere in life by wearing my heart on my sleeve.

Too bad he can't see me now.

I wear my heart on my sleeve and in the books I write.

Back then I simply tried to be less emotional when it came to helping employees with their problems. Grateful to be free of my past, I also started volunteering at a women's shelter for battered women. I thought I was strong enough to be able to use my experiences to help others going through what I did, but a few months after being there, I started having anxiety attacks and more night terrors. I had to resign from that work and focused my attentions on my family and our church life.

After seven years of renting houses, we finally bought our first little home, and things were good. It wasn't a big house nor in a fancy neighborhood, but it was new, and it was ours.

Then in our tenth year of marriage, we accepted a work assignment for Ben's job, and the company relocated us to China. I had matured into a confident woman in my mid-thirties and made a goal that while we were there, I'd take advantage of the break in my work life to learn to speak the language, write a book, and most special of all, I'd find a way to work with disadvantaged children.

It wasn't easy, but I finally found a way into the orphanage and started a volunteer group there. My work with the children changed my life. It was there that I found out who I really was and what my purpose in life was, feeling most passionate when I was able to use my skills to make the lives of the children better. I also took a position on the board of directors for the expatriate group and took over as their newsletter editor. I filled my life with goals and tasks, never wanting to be idle.

I probably took on too much, especially considering that in the first quarter of living there, I lost more than twenty pounds of my already lean frame. That first year in China was one of the hardest of my life, not only because of what I was witnessing in the orphanage but also because of the culture shock, the language barrier, and the feeling of being so far from everyone and everything that was familiar.

I missed my family desperately, and even though my twin sister and I have always had a tumultuous sisterhood, we had never been so far apart, and it was a strange and unsettling feeling to be unmoored from everything I knew.

In China, I tried to find a way to help animals, and one day, we happened upon a pet market where dogs, cats, and birds were shoved into tiny cages and suffering from heat and dehydration, sold for a paltry price.

There were two tiny Chinese pugs who I couldn't walk away from. One of them was being re-juiced with an IV for the afternoon shoppers to think he was healthy. It was obvious that both of them were sick.

I thought I could save them, so we brought them home.

What followed was three weeks of hell and tears while I tried to nurse little Max and Milo back to health from the nondiscriminating and lethal disease of Parvo.

We made daily trips to the vet clinic in town until the day that Milo was too far gone to keep punishing his little body. I sobbed and held him while they administered the drug that would set him free.

That night, I lay on the cold concrete floor in the bathroom with his brother who labored through vomiting and seizures until the next morning when I had to give him up as well.

Once again, I cried and held him, and when the final shot was given, there was just a few minutes of waiting, then I felt the most surreal *whoosh* flow through his body, and Max was gone.

That was the first and only time I ever felt that supernatural feeling of a spirit leaving its earthly body behind, though I would have to take one more China dog through the process.

This time, it was a puppy named Boomer who turned ferocious as a juvenile. After a scan proved his brain was damaged, probably from inbreeding (according to the vet), he had to be put down for the safety of others.

There were many afternoons that Boomer had cornered us, baring his fangs as he tried to bite. We would perch on the kitchen counter in terror, waiting for Ben to come home and pull the dog away so we could be safe.

Still, I grieved him too. It wasn't his fault that he was a product of inbreeding.

I stopped trying to save dogs over there and concentrated on just my work with the children. As a group, we were able to make huge changes that made their lives better. We raised money for lifesaving surgeries and expanded foster care to get as many out of the institution as we could and into family life. I also used my platform there to raise public awareness about adoption and foster care.

It was hard work, and I spent many nights awake, my insomnia at its worst while I ranted and raged at a God who would let those children suffer like I saw, some with health problems and others with neglect and abuse at the hands of their caretakers. For years I walked a thin line between wanting to explode with anger at the directors and knowing if I did, we'd be kicked out.

Eventually, a child who I loved deeply died because of their nonchalance about the severity of her condition, and I lost it. My spirit was broken, and even though they'd put me and my group in the same league that they did I. M. Pei, acknowledging us with a Pride of the

City award for humanitarian work, I was done.

After nearly five years in China, we returned home to South Carolina, and I later published a memoir detailing our adventures and trials from that time overseas. There was a lot of heartache in our journey but also many blessings, and we were lucky enough to be able to pursue Ben's love of travel.

We settled down and got back to American life. I took another job in human resources and was able to spearhead several community outreach programs. My favorite was our Zip Up the Warmth campaign. I remember how thankful I was so many years ago during a cold winter in Nebraska when my favorite teacher brought my siblings and me new coats.

I led our company employees in providing more than fifty new coats and backpacks to give to children in a needy neighborhood. The next thing I came up with was a Zip Up a Smile project in which I found a children's shelter that I toured then headed up a campaign to deliver them a hundred gallon-sized Ziploc bags with things a child needs when pulled out of their homes with no notice. A toothbrush, toothpaste, and other hygiene items, along with a journal for them to write their thoughts in, a small Bible to give them comfort, and finally, a set of warm pajamas for their first night away from home.

It was these little projects here and there that helped me grieve for my life in China and the children I left behind.

Two years later, we would move again for Ben's job. This time to Georgia where we were happy to find a high school that offered Chinese language studies. When we moved into our new home, our youngest daughter, Amanda, was struggling because all her best friends were left behind in China.

That was the life she knew the most, and she missed

it dearly.

We went to the shelter and got a cat. They called her Mama, but we named her Gypsy.

Gypsy was standoffish at first, but soon she was loving and a comfort to be around. I still thought Amanda needed more.

On our sixteenth wedding anniversary, Ben and I decided that instead of buying gifts for each other, we would get Amanda a dog. It would be her responsibility so that it would bond to her and be her new best friend.

She named him Max. Then Jake. And finally, I told her she had to set a permanent name, and she chose Riley. I added Radcliffe because he was a quiet, stoic little fellow that reminded me of a tiny professor. He filled Amanda's lonely spot for a while, but when she got her driver's license, everything changed, and she no longer had time to be Riley's best friend.

That meant he was suddenly all mine, and there couldn't have been a better time. Gypsy was a good cat, and I loved her dearly, but she wasn't one who seemed to care that I was struggling.

It had been years since I'd published my memoir, and I was working in human resources again and was doing volunteer administrative work for a foundation for Chinese children in orphanages, but my onslaught of chronic pain had pushed me into a depression.

My doctor put me through a battery of tests and diagnosed me but said overall that he believed years of trauma throughout my life had accumulated. And with all I had encountered in China with the loss of some of the children I loved, as well as my eldest daughter spiraling into troubled times, my body had had enough.

He said all my repressed emotions had to come out somehow.

When my chronic illness decided to show its ugly head, it became a monster. By then, I was an executive administrative assistant to the president of a company, and the pressure was so high I had to cut my hours back.

We only had Amanda at home there, and she was in high school. She also had a part-time job, started making friends, and was a busy preteen. When I got home after noontime from my job, I embraced having the house to myself so I could sleep.

Sleep, sleep, and sleep.

I could never get enough sleep.

During that time, Riley Radcliffe became my Velcro dog. Eventually I felt guilty that he was so happy to see me come home, only to see me fall into a stupor of despair. That intense need to always make a dog's life the best it can be got me off the couch.

Riley was my lifeline.

I want to say here that I still had a wonderful marriage to an amazing partner who tried to help me, and I was very grateful for that, but at that time, my husband's commute was three hours a day, and he worked ten hours.

He was gone a lot.

Riley became like the best counselor and balm of comfort a human could find. He was always such an intelligent dog, picking up on cues from me without a word. A natural hunter as a Yorkshire terrier, he also made me smile again with how seriously he took his efforts to keep all wildlife away from our home.

One afternoon, he was rustling through the shrubs while I sat on the porch reading. Suddenly he stood before me, proud in his capture of a little rabbit.

I screamed.

Then I jumped up and grabbed him. "Let it go, Riley Radcliffe! Let it go!"

I shook him, and he refused to let that rabbit go. The poor little thing was struggling like mad, but Riley held it tight. I was just sick over what the bunny was experiencing!

Finally, I held Riley over the banister and shook him. He was afraid of heights (like his mama) and immediately dropped the rabbit.

Unfortunately, by then the rabbit was stone silent, its eyes wide in death. I know it's probably stupid, but I cried.

I put Riley in the house and apologized to the bunny as I transferred his body to a box. I couldn't just leave him out there, or Riley would get him again. Or worse, Gypsy would find him and eat him.

We had a pond, and I thought about it for just a nanosecond then decided that would be terrible. I really didn't know what to do with it, so I put the box in my car and drove out.

With Ben on the phone, I drove while I told him about the terrible trauma I'd just been through in witnessing the death of an innocent creature by our bloodthirsty varmint.

He consoled me and told me to just pull over on the side of the road and set it out. I think he was more concerned about having a dead animal in our car. Just before I was ready to hang up the phone, my eyes wandered over to the box.

Suddenly, that dead rabbit jerked to life and jumped straight out of that box and onto the floor!

I screamed and nearly lost control of my car, trying to avoid the zombie rabbit from coming near me. Finally, I swerved over to the side of the road, slammed on the brake then jumped out of the car as fast as I could.

I got about thirty feet away when I realized no one was coming to save me, and I'd have to save myself.

And I needed a way home.

Quietly, so the rabbit wouldn't hear me coming, I sneaked up to the passenger side, and as though touching a hot stove, I grabbed the door handle and jerked open the door then jumped back at least ten feet.

"C'mon, little zombie bunny, come out of there," I pleaded. "Lord, don't make me touch it, don't make me touch it," I prayed.

My prayers were answered, and the rabbit peeked out the door, saw me, and jumped straight into the ditch then took off.

I won't even tell you about the incident with Riley and the chipmunk. It involved a broom. Enough said.

With Riley Radcliffe cheering me on and Gypsy snubbing my slowness, I began to recover. One day I rounded up the ambition I'd buried and decided to write my first novel.

But as soon as I made that decision, all those feelings of doubt crowded my mind.

Who do you think you are? You're a nobody. No extended education and no skills.

Miraculously, the memoir that had been unwanted by any publisher but was finally picked up was doing well. But it had been four years in which I had done nothing to capitalize on that success. I'd only written that book to tell the story of the children I knew and loved, who I promised I would speak for.

Writing a book is a hard thing, y'all.

Could I do it again?

My heart was always in writing, pouring out my feelings with the written word. But those were journals. Poetry.

Could I switch to writing novels?

I decided I'd never know unless I tried.

I put myself through the wringer writing that novel. I arrived an hour early to work to write every day and then wrote all afternoon when I got home, stopped to make supper then wrote until bedtime.

I put everything I had into the dream.

Ben was behind me the whole way, and together, we

decided to invest into the dream, using money we didn't have to build a website and other expenses.

During that time, I researched and thought I learned everything I needed to know to make the book a success before pitching it.

It was rejected.

I felt sad but not beaten.

I was angry, actually. I hadn't come so far in my life only to put my tail between my legs when someone said I wasn't good enough—or at least that was how I took it.

I went back to work and studied the market again then came up with a plan for another novel. I was determined that my same publisher would see the worth in me. I spent a year writing it then pitched the whole thing when it was completely done.

I held my breath.

It was accepted.

A Thread Unbroken, my very first novel, the story of two stolen girls in China and the father who refused to give up hope in finding them, was published.

My career was off and running. My social-network platforms began to gain ground, and realizing an opportunity to use it to do some good, I signed up for volunteer work in dog rescue. Using my reach of the network I was building, I was able to help find foster homes and new adoptive families for dogs in need.

Then I discovered a need in our county for CASAs, court-appointed special advocates for children in foster care. I signed up and went through the classes then took on my first case of a thirteen-year-old girl named Kathy, who was pulled out of her home. She said she'd heard voices in her head telling her to kill her parents. She was rebellious and unwilling to cooperate with anyone.

Everyone was afraid to be in a room alone with her after she'd picked up a metal folding chair and threw it at someone.

I marched into that room and introduced myself.

Alone.

Something about me and my modest background spoke to her, and we became friends. Though she was Hispanic, she truly reminded me of my eldest—and rebellious—daughter. I could relate to her and understand a lot of why she said and did the things she did.

Kathy always tried to put on a mean face, but one day, I traveled to where she was living in a group home and surprised her at school. I was waiting in the office when they called her up, and she thought she was in trouble. When she saw me standing there, she broke out in a huge smile and hugged me. The office lady said she'd never seen Kathy light up that way.

It was Kathy's birthday, and I wanted someone to acknowledge it for her, so I had gained permission to take her to the mall. I wasn't supposed to spend any money on gifts, but between you and me, she got a new jacket that day. Also a duffel bag, so she wouldn't have to carry her clothes to the next place in a garbage bag, along with a full set of hygiene items that every teen girl needs.

Yes, I used to break rules like those in the orphanage too.

Kathy and I had such a good talk that day, and she told me how much she missed her mom, a really hard confession for her. You see, Kathy's mom was older than the average mom. Much older. She couldn't speak English, but even at her advanced age, she supported her family with an extremely hard job at the chicken factory.

Even though her family had never been in this situation before, despite having raised four other daughters and Kathy being her youngest, the court system mandated that she take parenting classes. It was ridiculous.

But I am here to tell you, that woman was dedicated

to her kids and getting Kathy home. She took a bus and showed up to every single class then struggled through her shyness and the language barrier to fulfill the mandate.

She couldn't afford a lawyer, so she did what they told her to do to get her daughter back. She also showed up to every court date, looking fragile and afraid. She could've let Kathy languish in the system. It would have been easier for her.

She didn't.

And Kathy saw that dedication. She had lied about her family and admitted it, yet they did not give up on her. That's the kind of forgiveness I'd like to see more of.

I was proud to be Kathy's caseworker, and soon, getting her home where she wanted to be was my first priority and goal. I began to feel like, even though my work in the orphanage was over, I was starting to do something good with my life again.

On the other hand, with working my job, writing a book, and being a CASA with frequent court dates, home/school visits, and tons of paperwork, Ben thought I was pushing myself too hard. He was right, but it was what I'd always done, and I couldn't change that about myself. After two years of battling social services, in which they'd sometimes lie outright and after Kathy admitted to the judge that there were no voices, that she was just going through a rebellious period, we got her home.

The day in court when they were declared reunified was one of the most emotional days I've ever had. I doubt that Kathy will ever take her mother for granted again.

With that case resolved, they handed me my next one. A grandmother was fighting her daughter for custody of her toddler grandchildren for their safety. The day that I had to make my home visit, the woman was so worried.

She lived in a tiny little trailer on the outskirts of town. When she let me in, she kept apologizing for her home.

Though it was small, it was clean. She had places made for the babies and homemade rugs and other things around. There were toys but not so many to be overwhelming. The furniture was threadbare, and it looked like she had to make every penny stretch.

It was perfect.

And I told her so.

For what I saw in that house was better than expensive furniture and lots of square footage. There was a grandmother that would use her last breath to protect her grandchildren, and there was love.

Lots of it.

I recommended to the judge that yes, she should get custody. And after many court sessions, she did.

I quit my job and focused on writing and my volunteer work.

The best part about it was that I could do most of it from a chair sitting right beside my little furry bestie.

Soon after that, I would get a three-book deal with a fancy-schmancy advance that allowed me to buy our youngest daughter a better car and do more to help out my eldest daughter with her children. I was proud.

I had found me again.

And my stoic and loyal Riley Radcliffe was the biggest reason for that.

21

THE DAPPER GENTLEMAN

Eventually, when Amanda graduated high school, we bounced back from Georgia to South Carolina again into a lovely little lake cabin on Hartwell. Nothing fancy or over the top, just a small house with a path to the lake, but we were happy there. We spent weekends fishing and boating and had cookouts with family finally around. It was a fun home for Amanda to visit from college, joining her friends for sunning on the lake and probably a lot of other stuff I didn't need to know about.

The grandkids loved it, too, especially the hot tub, which they thought was just a pool their size. We were content there for a long time. Then we started to get the urge for another adventure.

After much research, we took a relocation tour to Panama in Central America and loved what we found. We were longing to add some zest to our life, and we started planning to move there. We sold everything—our home, boat, furniture.

Most of it was gone quickly in one big yard sale for pennies on the dollar of what we paid, except the house, which we made back our money on but no real profit to speak of.

I had fun during this season because there is nothing I like better than purging and organizing, and the task of emptying out our life to make room for something brand-new was fun for me.

To ready for the move, I asked a very good friend to adopt my cat, Gypsy, then flew her to Texas and settled her into her new home. I cried all the way back to the east coast.

Then everything felt apart when I found out that my eldest daughter had turned to drugs. In the stress of that discovery, my health took another dive.

A deep, deep dive.

I spent weeks on the phone until I finally got through to one woman, a doctor's wife, who agreed to let my daughter into their outpatient program if I would pay fully up front.

That was my first effort in helping her.

I would later go in for a skin biopsy on spots that I suspected might be melanoma, only to find out instead that it was positive for a mast cell disease called masto-cytosis. I'd never heard of it, but it was the answer to a life full of muscle and bone pain, along with a lot of other frustrating symptoms like migraines and digestive issues.

After a bone biopsy, it was confirmed to only be cuta-neous thus far but can one day go systemic, affecting my organs and possibly leading to an earlier death.

We decided that we needed our company-sponsored health insurance, and our Panama dream was called off. Ben would need to work in his position until retirement age. We were both disappointed, to say the least. I think we were itching for a new, crazy adventure, but at least we would be able to stick around and try to be a positive influence in our grandchildren's lives.

Because we'd already sold our home, that meant we had to find something else.

By the time that we moved onto our farm of nearly forty acres, way out in South Carolina country, we'd been married twenty-five amazingly happy years.

In my wandering life, I'd lived in more than four dozen homes, on two continents, and in towns across many states from coast to coast in the USA. Together as a couple, we'd made memories in Mexico, Thailand, Malaysia, China, Philippines, Central America, Bahamas, and Australia. We'd put two children through college then worked hard to pay off all our bills (except for our home) and were saving a little bit of money.

Both of us were doing well in our careers only by the grace of God and because we lifted each other up all along the way, through good times and bad, never wavering in our love and admiration for each other, and our goal of building a legacy for our family.

Sure, we'd been hit with some heartbreaking things, just like other families, but we supported one another to make it through. I think the key to our happiness is that we have always tried to keep our marriage a love story. However, I was tired of moving around. The farm was nice, but it was Ben's dream. Lots of land. A couple tractors. All the things that reminded him of his childhood, and I was happy to see him get it, considering how hard he'd always worked.

We settled into the log cabin with Riley Radcliffe and Kaiser and sometimes my youngest daughter's dog, Griffin. We got up close and personal with all sorts of wildlife, including deer, coyotes, skunks, wild pigs, and more.

I'll never forget the day that Ben said he'd had enough of the skunk that was visiting us every night. He took his dad's long gun (I have no idea what it's called), and as I peeked out the kitchen window, I watched him creep around the house looking like Elmer Fudd.

I was literally laughing at the scene as he tried to sneak

up behind the skunk that was making his way down our driveway.

Ben shot the gun.

Just like in a cartoon, a little puff of vapor rose over the skunk, and it skedaddled into the tree line.

I was glad that my Elmer missed the shot. And the skunk didn't come back.

While we lived on the farm, Amanda was in her last year of college and decided to pursue her dream of working in Hawaii.

After some intense interviewing sessions, she snagged a job on Maui. We helped her get a new start over there, and we were thrilled for her, but that left me feeling empty in a home without her to mother over.

My eldest daughter was still in a struggle of her own and blaming me for all her problems, so she wasn't coming around. Yes, we had our grandkids, but it was quite a trek up and down the interstate with a day of driving, and we were always last on their schedules at the holidays, if at all.

That meant we were to have our first Christmas season with a completely empty nest, other than our fur-kids at the farm.

I didn't know what to do with myself without being the mom who coordinates Christmas. I canceled all festivities because I wanted to wallow in the black cloud that was chasing me and threatening to envelop me in its dark embrace.

I fought it, but it was winning. Then one afternoon, a week before the big day, Ben and I decided to go take a drive, just to get out of the house. It was raining and bitter cold, and I didn't really feel like doing anything except snuggling in my own warm bed, but I also didn't want to disappoint him.

Ironically, he wasn't thrilled about going anywhere either. We were doing it for each other, out of care for the other's feelings.

In the car, we cruised around, wasting time until we turned to head for home. At the usual fork in the road, Ben said, "We've never been down this road before. Let's see what's there."

I didn't care. I was quiet, staring out my window and feeling a bit sorry for myself.

Then, in the side mirror, I saw a tiny little head pop up out of the ditch and look around.

"Stop the car," I said.

"Why?"

"I think I just saw a little dog in that high grass."

He stopped and, at my insistence, started backing the car up.

"There he is." I was out of the car before it had even completely stopped.

Coincidentally, it was a Yorkie, the same breed of dog that I volunteered for in rescue. His hair was matted and tangled, completely covering one eye. I could also see a few bald spots around his ear.

He looked like he'd been lost for a very long time.

I knelt down and talked to him. He didn't run. Instead, he seemed relieved to see me, and when I asked if he needed help, he pranced right over and let me pick him up.

"Oh, honey," Ben said. "He's old. And in bad shape."

"I know. That's why we can't leave him here," I replied. "It's supposed to freeze tonight. He won't survive it."

Then we got a whiff of what smelled worse than death on the scrawny little fellow.

Ben held his nose. "We cannot put him in our car. The smell would never come out."

We all know how that went over. I stood in the street holding that pitiful critter and told my husband that I'd walk the five miles home.

In the rain.

With the dog.

Sighing in frustration, he let me hold the dog on my lap after promises that I'd only get him medical help and try to find his family for him.

The dog sat up in my lap like a perfect gentleman. He looked straight ahead out the window as if to say, "Finally. I thought you'd never show up."

He was ready to go.

We arrived home, and because Ben was afraid he might be contagious with something that could hurt our pack, I took the dog down to the guesthouse. Then I brought down some premium wet dog food, and he ate like he was ravenous.

Every tiny morsel. He followed that up with long gulps of fresh water.

Then I made him a bed in a box, using the softest thing I could find for bedding. It was my daughter's robe, which was fitting since I was missing her so much.

The dog didn't even hesitate. He jumped into that box and settled down in the warmth of the robe then closed his eyes and went to sleep.

My heart shifted a little because I could tell that the little fellow was just happy to have a full belly and a warm bed.

The next morning, I was dreading what I would find in the guesthouse. My biggest fear was that the dog would've died during the night. My second worry was that he had probably exploded with accidents all over the floor.

When I opened the door, the dog greeted me with prancing around my legs, his tongue hanging out the side of his mouth in a gleeful smile.

There wasn't one single accident anywhere.

He truly was a perfect little gentleman.

I fed him then took him straight to the veterinarian,

who told me that he appeared to be a senior male dog, at least twelve to fourteen years old, and in horrible health. Barely four pounds, he was tangled, matted, covered in fleas, and so very skinny that you could see every rib. His jaw also appeared to be a little sideways, probably an old injury that healed on its own, the vet said.

Unfortunately, he also had severe gingivitis and not too many teeth either. His mouth was full of painful pus pockets that needed to be treated before the teeth could be seen to. The vet said it was obvious he had not been on a normal diet and had scavenged to stay alive, which later became apparent as he passed all the sticks and leaves he'd been eating.

The vet asked me how much I wanted to put into his care since he was a stray and very old and maybe too close to starvation to save. I replied, "Whatever it takes to make him comfortable." I didn't want him to be in any pain, and I was glad that I'd found him to at least end his suffering.

The vet said that the dog was too fragile to give him the rabies or any other vaccine, but he shot him up with antibiotics then gravely told me he probably wouldn't live long.

The groomer had to shave him to free him of the tangles and fleas then bathe him three consecutive times. His toenails looked as though they'd been growing for a decade, and they took care of those too.

During all the handling, this little fellow was quiet and patient, standing there with a proud but hopeful look in his eyes. An expression that said, "This isn't easy, but it's okay because I know you are trying to help me."

The veterinarian and I marveled over the coincidence for Ben and I to have taken a drive that day and turn down a road we'd never been on, only to find the exact kind of dog that I represented in our rescue.

Or was it more than a coincidence?

I took him home. A tiny shell-shocked and eerily quiet little fellow who didn't even have the strength to bark or climb onto the couch. At first, we called him Oliver, but he was the epitome of a sweet old grandpa, so that was what his name came to be. Grandpa ate very well but otherwise slept most of the time, snuggled into the softest and warmest thing I could find, my beloved pashmina scarf from our trip overseas.

I still missed having my youngest daughter close, but it helped that I devoted every minute of the holidays to caring for Grandpa. I pushed my melancholy away as I concentrated on making him feel safe and loved, determined to let him live long enough to know love before he died.

We got through Christmas.

During this time, I posted his photo on every lost dog site I could find so that if someone was out there looking for him, they could be reunited.

We had a lot of possible connections, but none of them

panned out to be his real family.

Because we were at full capacity and dealing with our own trauma pup, I tried to fulfill my promise and find him a new home to live out what might only be weeks or months of the rest of his life. We tried two new places, but they didn't work out, and I brought him back both times, silently thankful for more time to love on him.

Then he got sick. Very sick with vomiting and bloody diarrhea every day, leaving bloody trails of it through the house if we couldn't get him outside fast enough.

It was terrifying, but we didn't give up. Instead, we spent a lot of time at the clinic until, with much research on both our parts, Grandpa was diagnosed with CIL, Canine Intestinal Lymphangiectasia, a protein-losing disease that is sometimes called a "wasting disease" and when discovered can result in a prognosis of less than two years, depending on severity.

That began a journey of intense research as we tried to find a diet Grandpa could handle. We tried many things before resorting to home cooking, and finally, we hit upon the right combination of cooked meals.

While I continued to look for the perfect home, Grandpa was changing. With a new, strict diet, he was gaining strength, and he found his voice again. He could even hop up on the furniture without assistance. Grandpa also found joy in following around my pups, attaching himself to Riley Radcliffe as his closest buddy and comrade.

Our little gentleman began to understand the affection I poured on him was a good thing, and he wanted more, always coming to me to be tucked into my sweater for a little nap.

Soon I could see my Ben trying not to show that he was warming up to our little Grandpa. It was hard not to, as the little guy just oozed friendliness and forgiveness for the way humans had treated him so far.

At the same time that Grandpa was building a huge fan base around the world through all the photos and stories I posted about him, he was finding his place in the pack. He began to have a great time gallivanting around our huge, fenced yard with Riley, sniffing out critters. We even caught him eating a bird once, and we lectured him and assured him he'd never go hungry again. He made us laugh daily with his bobbing tail and the long tongue that always hung out the side of his mouth. And he was so very eager to please! To belong! We found out that his age was actually a plus because he was much lower key and more affectionate than a younger dog.

But we both agreed that we just couldn't handle another dog, especially one that was so old and would have many needs.

But then Grandpa and I had a moment.

It was more special than all the others put together. I

had taken him out into the cold air one morning to potty, and when he was done, he ran back to me. I tucked him into my sweater to bring him in and once inside, I decided to keep him there for a few minutes to warm his skinny bones. We sat down in the rocking chair, and he tucked his little head under my chin and burrowed deeper, even closer to my chest.

Usually he was fairly stiff, unsure of being dropped or who knows what else. But this time, I felt his body begin to slowly relax. Soon he began a soft little snore, and I looked down and saw total contentment on his sleepy face. I realized that I might just be the first human he completely trusted and was willing to let his guard down with.

I just melted.

That sweet, trust-filled moment was all I needed to convince me that Grandpa had already found his home. (And he wants everyone to know that rescuing older dogs is a gift and not a chore. Like him, he knows that the senior pups who have nearly given up hope only need someone to give them a chance. Let them in, and they'll show you that you won't be rescuing them because they will rescue you first.)

As months flew by with our debonair little gentleman, my eyes were opened to what a blessing rescuing a senior can be. Grandpa could never be called high maintenance, for all he really required was snuggles and lap time, and he was so grateful for every little thing that a younger dog may take for granted. Some of his favorite moments were with the family walks, which sometimes tired him out enough that he rode back in my little satchel, held against my body with his tiny head peeked out, watching as we went.

Sometimes I just watched him and wondered where he had been and who had loved him. I knew he probably had some great stories! There were coyotes and hawks all around where we found him, and he must have been a cunning and determined little fellow in order to stay alive for so many years.

I must confess here now that I finally got some reliable information about where Grandpa came from. A volunteer for another rescue just across the state line contacted me and said she knew who he was. She didn't know his name, but she had seen him when called out to the place to pick up another dog the family had relinquished. The volunteer told me to take everything down that was public about him because he should never be returned to them.

She stated that she'd seen him in their yard and noticed he was malnourished and had a jaw injury. She had pleaded with the woman to let the rescue take him too but was refused.

Now everything made total sense. The road that we found Grandpa coming out of the ditch on was very close to a chicken farm. He also smelled worse than death. Most telling, though, was the fact that at night, he had a routine where he would strut around the house and make noises in the back of his throat that sounded just like a chicken! He would look in all the corners of every room, and if he found a bug, he'd snatch it up and eat it.

Grandpa thought he was a chicken!

It really broke my heart to think he had spent probably most of his time outside with the chickens, scavenging for whatever he could to stay alive. I agreed with the whistleblower. He was going nowhere.

As we set out to give Grandpa the best retirement anyone could ask for, it was fun for us to see him begin to mimic the pack and behave like a dog. Well, sort of a chicken-dog, but he tried, and the other pups gave him the respect he deserved. To me, he was five pounds of pure sugar, but to them, he was the leader of the pack.

Grandpa also loved riding the John Deere Gator with us. He claimed the prime spot on Mama's lap while the other boys were in the back. Each night we took them riding around the trails on our land, watching for deer, rabbits, and the random big box turtles that lived around there.

One time the boys all got a big surprise right along with us when a mama wild pig saw us and sounded the alarm. She took off down a huge ravine, all five of her little piglets following obediently. Another evening, we scared up a lovely little fawn hiding in the brush.

Grandpa was such a gentle creature that he never thought to try to get after the wildlife, except if we'd hear coyotes in the distance at night, and then he'd huddle somewhere. I supposed in his travels he'd hid from them too many times to count.

On those rides around the farm, he looked so proud, surveying the land with us that he thought of as his too.

At the time that we had Grandpa, we also had a little

foster failure named Kaiser, a troubled boy relinquished to the rescue I volunteer for by a woman who met me in the parking lot of a restaurant. His owner only had terrible things to say about him and was glad to get him off her hands. She called him a junkyard dog and said he had no manners. He was definitely a trauma pup, and we could tell that he had probably been put into a pen or crate and left there for long periods of time. He also had an untreated eye injury that she said he got in a fight with the neighbor's pit bull.

The first day after he came to live with us, I took him to the veterinarian, and he was like a bucking bronco at the end of my leash. I could barely control him, and when it came time for his exam, he climbed me like a tree and tried to hide behind my neck. We decided to keep our Kamikaze Kaiser with us so that we could try to save his eye, which after nearly two years of costly care had to go anyway.

Our Kaiser boy took living on the farm very seriously, and he also lived for the rides around the property. Though the boys were always harnessed in, there was one time we didn't know that Kaiser had wiggled out of his harness until his stout, chubby self came running frantically up beside us as though to say, "Hey! Let me back on!"

Ben slammed on the brakes, and we laughed like crazy.

Kaiser also had what we referred to as his girlfriend. It was a sturdy stuffed animal that he would hump several times a day. I talked to a behavioral vet who said that was his way of easing his anxiety. Unfortunately, his anxiety seemed to increase when we had company over, making for some interesting dinnertime entertainment. Eventually he calmed down enough that he only needed an after-dinner session, and that was enough to keep him somewhat neutral.

Sometimes Kaiser reminded us of the penguin in Batman. He was something else. It took a lot of time and effort, but we were able to help him with a lot of his issues.

Grandpa was instrumental in that, always bringing a sense of calm in the moments that Kaiser was acting out. Eventually though, Kaiser backslid into his trauma behavior. He began attacking Riley Radcliffe and left him seriously injured more than a few times.

After several visits and prescriptions that went nowhere in helping Kaiser's issues, the veterinarian recommended he be euthanized. I could not do that, so after seeking the perfect placement, I found that connection through my good friend, Karen.

We made arrangements, and my other friend, Michelle, and I drove Kaiser to a lovely couple in Arkansas to live the life he deserved with a ranch manager and his bride.

Even though I knew it was for the best, when we left Kaiser behind, I cried my heart out. We stopped at a hotel somewhere (it's a blur now), and that night, we ate a quick dinner in the restaurant. I'm not a drinker (I think I've said that before), but I decided to have something to help me calm down. I can't remember if there was peer pressure or not, but for the sake of my defense, let's just assume there was.

I was shocked that with every sip of that drink, I was forgetting how terribly guilty I felt, so I ordered another. I'm pretty sure there were three in total, but whatever it was, we had to get an escort from the front desk to get us up the elevator and to the right room. I don't remember the rest of the night except for Michelle making me laugh hysterically when she was in the bathroom and I yelled out to ask her if she was flossing.

She came out, flossing her teeth and doing the floss dance that was so popular during that time. Michelle is a speech pathologist and works with children, so she always knows what's new. She's also the absolute best friend to take on a soul-crushing journey with you when you know you are going to need some light moments to keep you from jumping off a building.

To see her standing there between the beds, floss in her mouth while she did the floss-dance moves, was too much for my rarely inebriated brain. Soon the hysterical laughter turned back to tears, and I was crying over Kaiser again, then it got deep, and I was pouring out my feelings over the ongoing troubled relationship with my mother.

Michelle finally put me to sleep. Probably with a pillow over my head to drown out the pity party, but we'll never know.

The next morning while she was in the shower, I snuck off to find a drugstore and bought something for nausea.

Lesson learned.

Don't drink.

Michelle will tell you that even though I thought I drowned my tears away the night before, I still cried nearly the entire ride home. But I'm happy to say that it has been two years now, and Kaiser's new pack mom and dad have made Kaiser into a happy and well-adjusted only fur-child, except for his brother, the one-legged pirate bird named Hoppie, who I pray doesn't get eaten one day by a crazy one-eyed dog.

Kaiser now gets all the attention he needs and sometimes more. I smile when I read of his antics and see photos of him after tangling with a skunk or hear of his altercation with a cow or see him sitting on his pack dad's lap as he thinks he is driving. He has such a unique—and needy—personality, and it's hard to believe that a professional wanted to snuff that out of him.

Back at the farm, we soon brought a little foster girl into our home, and Grandpa made me laugh at how he treated her like a spoiled granddaughter. Primrose and her puppy were two dogs pulled out of a hellacious situation with a pack of other Yorkies. I was not there during the actual rescue, but the pictures alone of the state of the house they were hoarded in could turn your stomach.

I only volunteered to foster one dog from the group, but when I went to pick one, I saw how much more terrified Primrose was than the rest of them and knew I had to bring her to my quiet environment to heal. Of course, I couldn't take her away from her pup, so I also scooped up the little one and named her Bitsy Braveheart.

Where Primrose was frightened and nervous of everything, her puppy—a tiny blur of barely three pounds—was a fireball of courage.

It was a long car ride, and they were both terrified and crying. For four hours on the road, I tried to comfort them with soft music and whispers of words. When I finally got them home, I brought the crate inside and unlocked the door, allowing them to come out at their own pace.

Bitsy shot out like a cannonball, ready to see who and what we were all about.

But her mama would not come out.

As a matter of fact, when I finally tried to lift her out, she spread all four legs like a flying squirrel and tried to cling to the bars, resisting my efforts in her panic to stay out of reach.

Because of her trauma, I relented and left her there, with the door open as an invitation.

Finally, she got hungry and quietly slipped out.

I set up a playpen, and she and the baby stayed in there a lot for the first few days. I'd put Grandpa in with them for short periods, and he seemed to comfort them and bring Primrose a sense of safety. When I had housetrained the puppy and gotten her to completely trust humans again, it was time to take her to her new home.

It broke my heart to separate her from her mama, but Primrose had gotten to the point where she was snapping at the puppy and trying to stay away from her. Bitsy was too brave and rambunctious to handle when everything else was scary to Primrose.

We hit the road, and our little foster Bitsy Braveheart went to one of the most loving homes I've ever visited. Her two dads were so grateful they'd been picked to have her that there were tears. Almost instantly, Bitsy bonded with them and became their little Noodles, and along with her fur-siblings, Mrs. Wiggles and Butters, is still a vital part of their family pack.

The first night that Primrose didn't have her puppy with her, she cried until I finally lifted her out of the pen and put her next to me in the bed. She snuggled up next to my chest in the curve of my neck. All through the night, I kissed her and whispered words of comfort to her. I think I turned her into a little kissy monster because then she came out of her shell and wanted to kiss everyone in the pack, all the time! Especially on the top of her kissing list each day was Riley Radcliffe, who she had an obviously major crush on.

Sometimes she would run up to him and start kissing him all over his face, and Grandpa would approach them as though he was their chaperone.

Grandpa loved her, too, and even offered her some of his prime real estate on my lap when we did our rides around the property.

Primrose was a little doll, and it was hard, but she eventually went to live with her forever mom and pack of two more doggos. That was a hard one because Primrose wouldn't let anyone but me hold her. How would anyone love her and kiss her like I did? When I left her, I hurried out of the subdivision and then pulled over and draped myself over the steering wheel, sobbing uncontrollably.

I prayed to God, asking if I'd done the right thing. Right then, a text came through.

I looked at it, and it was from Primrose's new mama.

A photo of Primrose sleeping against her chest as Jessie rocked her to sleep. It was truly miraculous, and it filled me with relief. I still slept with Primrose's pink diaper under my pillow for weeks, just until I could get over not having her snuggled against me at night.

I do have it on good authority that Primrose became the leader of her new pack and still gets to enjoy nightly kisses in the bed, snuggled up with her mom and sister, Posey. Grandpa was also sad to see her go, but the silver lining was he got all of my lap back.

As Grandpa completely accepted our love and respect, he was truly the leader of the pack and proud of that position too. He began to walk with his head held high and a swagger in his step. But he was still sweet and loving. There were very rare times that I saw him get sassy because that was just not who he was, but if he needed to break up a squabble, he would prance right over there and do it. And they would listen.

Grandpa had two really good years with us, and then he began to decline again. At the time, we were building a house, and my prayers were that he would be able to make it until he got to live in the new home with us so that it would have his imprint there as well.

He held on, and after we moved in, we brought in another trauma foster pup named Rango, a young dog with a lot of issues.

To begin with, Rango was skin and bones, just teetering on the edge of starvation. In addition to a skin issue that made his muzzle nearly hairless, he also had double ear infections and an upper respiratory infection. He'd been found wandering the streets, his tail a pus-filled infected and mangled mess. The vet said the old injury had gone into necrosis and had to come off, so it was amputated all the way down.

Emotionally, we could tell that Rango was used to a lot of self-soothing. Out of nowhere, he would fall into an anxiety attack and start twirling as fast as he could. You could just feel the anxiety building inside him, and he would spin until he tired out, then go and stare at the wall or the ceiling.

Grandpa began to go and lay next to Rango at some of those high-anxiety moments as though telling him "it's okay, little fellow. I'm here, and we've got this."

Rango became a permanent part of the Bratt Pack in part because we fell completely head over heels in love with his silly nature. Also, because many times a dog with such deep issues could get bounced around, and we did not want that to happen to him.

In our home, we could take as much time as we needed to love him and make him feel that he never had to worry again. I'm glad to report that though Rango will always have recurring ear issues that we treat nearly constantly, his skin issues have cleared, and he's a handsome, healthy boy who rarely twirls these days. In the early days, he didn't quite know how to take touch from us, but now he's the best hugger out of the bunch. When he leans in, he falls all over you, and you can feel the love.

However, Rango is of the rescue variety that he has to have plenty of exercise to burn off the anxiety, or it can get pent up and cause problems. He has also been known to escape and take off throughout the neighborhood, leading us on a wild chase and earning himself the nickname of Runaway Rango.

In our new home, winter began to arrive, and Grandpa was declining even more. It was getting harder for us to talk him into eating, even as we sat on the floor and tried to coax him with all manners of home-cooked meals. He had attacks at night where he could not get his breath, and he would jump off the bed in a terrified state, trying to outrun the suffocation that he was feeling. It was horrific to have to stand by and watch him struggle and talk him calmly through the incidents.

We began to prepare ourselves, and even though I didn't want to face the truth, I also did not want him to suffer any longer.

One day when the sun was shining high in the sky and the temperatures were a bit on the warmer side, I bundled Grandpa up, and we took him on a boat ride. I knew we would be on the lake all summer with our pack, and he would not be with us, so I wanted to have that moment together.

As we cruised slowly along the water, I held my little gentleman in my arms and barely said a word. I think that Grandpa knew the ride was a symbolic gesture between him and me because he didn't even try to get out of the little warm bundle. Instead, he snuggled against me and quietly watched the reflection of the sun bouncing off the water like a parade of sparkling diamonds.

It was another two or three months before I could make the decision.

Every day leading up to his last, I prayed for a miracle. But finally, I called to make the appointment. I was sobbing so hard, but the girl at the front desk also loved our little old man, so she knew what I couldn't get out in words. She made the appointment for the following Monday.

That gave us the weekend.

On that final day, I held him a lot. We sat out on the back porch, and I rocked him against me in the way that always brought us both such comfort. I told Riley and Rango what was happening, but they didn't seem to understand.

When Ben arrived home, we dressed Grandpa in his favorite little collared shirt, bundled him up with his blanket, and headed to the clinic.

With Grandpa on my lap, cradled in his bed, I stared out the car window and let silent tears rain down my face. I wanted to be strong for my little guy, but I could not turn off the fountain. Ben tried to comfort me with words and kept reaching for my hand, but we both knew the hardest part was yet to come.

Because of COVID-19, no one was supposed to be allowed into the clinic, but we got permission from our doctor to break the rules. There was no way I could hand Grandpa off to a stranger for his last moments on Earth.

Masked and gloved, we entered the clinic, took him in, and they showed us to a private room. The doctor came in and gave the first shot then gave us some time.

Ben and I took turns holding Grandpa and talking to him.

As I rocked him back and forth in the way I know he loved, I relayed to him how much joy he had brought to me. I thanked him for getting me through the first few years of having my youngest child so far away.

Because all of the dogs feel more secure in their dad's arms, I finally relented my hold on Grandpa and turned him over to Ben, who quietly told our sweet boy that it was okay to go, that he would feel much better, and we would be fine without him.

That last part was a lie.

For the first time, I saw my husband cry over a dog. My husband is a big macho kind of fellow who is my rock, but tears ran down his face during his own goodbye to the smallest creature with the biggest heart we had ever known.

I am sad that I couldn't send Grandpa off with joy, as I had intended, but it just wasn't possible. The pain of those minutes is still so heavy in my heart, but I want people to know that when they're saying goodbye to their beloved pets, try to send them out with positive thoughts and thankfulness.

And please, please do not ever say you are not strong enough to be there.

They have been there for you through everything. Do not let them down in their final moments. Send them out with love and thankfulness and tell them that you will see them again. If your health is a factor in taking your pet in, try to find a veterinarian who will come to your home so the last minutes can be spent together.

When Grandpa's spirit left him, we tucked him into his little bed and handed him off to the vet tech. With ragged sobs, I begged her to make sure he kept his blanket and bed so that he could be warm as he made his transition.

She was kind and assured me that she would.

When I announced his passing, there were people all around the world who had never met him in person but had loved Grandpa from afar who cried right along with me. He touched so many hearts and inspired many to give a senior rescue pup a chance. For such a tiny guy, his legacy was huge.

A week later, I received Grandpa's ashes and his footprint made in plaster. They now sit in a place of honor on my bookshelf, next to the tiny hat we used to make him honorary sheriff of the Bratt Pack. My dad also traveled to our new home and planted a weeping willow tree in Grandpa's honor, and we have a small memorial stone there.

I won't say I was strong in the days after his death.

Grandpa was different to me than the other dogs that I have had in the sense that he filled a motherly need for me to have something living, breathing, and tiny to hold at a time when I felt I was losing my identity as a mother.

Some of my best memories were of me rocking Grandpa to sleep, giving him comfort as I took it from him as well. With his loss, there was a huge hole in my heart, and it felt like others just didn't understand how big it was. So, if you are feeling the same way as you read this, please know that I understand, and I know your pain.

I could end the story there, but instead I'm going to share something very special with you. In my hope that this book will bring you comfort, I've decided I have to be one hundred percent transparent in my experiences and my beliefs.

A few nights after Grandpa died, it was after midnight, and in my drowsy state, I heard the peck of his nails walking across the floor. I have three fur-boys, and I know which one of them it is without looking, just by their pace and the weight of the sounds.

When I heard what I knew without a doubt was Grandpa's walk, his nails hitting the floor, I sat up in bed and looked around. Rango lay at my feet, snoring. I reached under the bed on my side to feel Riley, as he usually was there all night. And yes, he was there. Sleeping.

Grandpa was the one who wandered that night.

And I am positive I heard him.

Tricia Flippin, my dog-rescue partner tells this of her experience in hearing her beloved dog come to her one night.

My baby, Casey, went to Heaven in 2016. He was fifteen years old and always slept on a pillow above my head in the bed. I still sleep with his pillow above my head, and a few nights after he left, I was lying in bed and heard his footsteps walk across the bedroom floor. My other boys, Romi and Cocoa, were lying next to me in the bed, so I know it wasn't them. I have since heard the same thing several times over the years and have even heard him come up the steps to get on the bed.

It seems hearing a departed dog visiting in the night is more common than one would think. Still, I needed to know more. I went on Amazon and bought several research books. After reading *Signs from the Universe* by Laura Lynne Jackson, I was still grieving and needed to know that Grandpa was in a good place and, most of all, not gone from me forever.

Because the book says you need to ask for something specific, I told him to show me a black butterfly. I have seen all kinds of gold and other colors of butterflies around our place but never black. That would be my irrefutable proof.

No more than two days later, I was on the porch calling in the dogs after a potty break. I called out, "C'mon boys!" and held the door open, like I always do. Riley ran in first. Then Rango. Then, right before my very eyes, a black butterfly.

Straight into the house.

Immediately, without hesitation, I said, "Well, hello, Grandpa."

I shut the door and turned to look for the butterfly. I

wanted to see it again. I wanted a photo! But the black butterfly was nowhere to be found. Where had it gone in less than a minute? It had disappeared, but in its place was a very warm feeling of peace and comfort.

A week after that, I doubted myself. Perhaps it was probably just coincidence.

Then one day, I was standing in line at the post office and looked out toward the street.

In the big window, I saw a black butterfly beating its wings frantically against the pane. I felt sorry for it and hoped that someone else coming through the door would grab him and toss him outside. As I moved up the line, I kept watch and saw four different people walk past the butterfly without even noticing it. I could hear the beating of the wings from where I stood ten feet away. How could they not hear it when they were within inches? Then I watched as the butterfly flew high up into the top of the window, at least fifteen feet from the floor. I told myself if it came back down to where I could reach him by the time I got finished at the counter, I'd rescue him.

I spent more time than usual at the counter, as I had a lot of book mail to send out. By the time I turned around to go to the exit, I had forgotten all about the butterfly. But I saw him instantly, now completely motionless and sitting at the bottom of the windowsill, as though waiting for me.

I stood in front of him and smiled.

Hi, Grandpa, I whispered.

The customer line was long again, and I could see that people were watching me curiously. I knew I looked a little bit over the top, but because I didn't want to hurt the butterfly's wings, I went to the garbage can and rustled through until I found a used paper coffee cup.

In order to get the butterfly, I had to lay down my purse on the writing counter. I then took the cup to the window and gently scooped up the butterfly, using my hand to cover the top once I had him so that he couldn't fly back into the window.

Leaving my purse behind, I carried the cup to the door.

I could've just tossed the butterfly into the air, but I saw a nice area down at the street that was level with a tree with some green space. So, holding the cup with one hand and using the other to cover it, I went down the long stairs.

Once I got near the tree, I took my hand away.

The butterfly flew up then dipped back down for a minute then was up, up, and away.

Silently, I thanked the universe for the gift, a peaceful balm to my broken heart.

Two black butterflies within a matter of days

22

———◆———

IN LOVING MEMORY OF GRANDPA OLIVER

Grandpa Oliver, a dapper Yorkshire gentleman of the official Bratt Pack, died peacefully alongside his mom of just over two years, under the care of a trusted veterinary hospital staff.

Grandpa grew up on a chicken farm in Georgia and was adopted by his pack mom, Kay Bratt, at the ripe age of at least fourteen years old, after she found him making his getaway toward the state line on a cold and rainy December day.

Grandpa quickly became something that legends are made of, embracing his creature-neutral role of both dog and chicken and taking his place as the honorary sheriff of Windy Hill, a sprawling thirty-eight-acre farm just far enough from his old home that his past couldn't catch up to him. Grandpa took his security job very seriously and made a point to keep guard against coyotes and wild pigs but was also known to enjoy a nice comfy lap and rocking in front of a warm fire wearing his favorite sweater.

Grandpa will be greatly missed by many but none more so than his mom, who believes that he was sent to her as a gift to help her through the pain of an empty nest. Grandpa leaves behind three brothers: Riley

Radcliffe, Kamikaze Kaiser, and Runaway Rango. He also leaves behind three foster sisters who have gone on to their forever homes: Primrose, Noodles, and Clarabelle, as well as the many chickens who knew and loved him in Georgia.

At the wishes of Grandpa's family, he would be honored if you reached out a helping hand to senior dogs, who still have the capacity to steal a heart or two. Donations to a rescue that takes in "old dogs" would also be appreciated. Lastly, Grandpa says that if you look hard and trust with your heart, you can find him in the gentle flutter of a black butterfly's wings.

23

MY HAPPILY EVER AFTER

Do you remember when I told you that I stopped into the church I'd never been to, just my little daughter and me, and broke down to the words of "I Surrender All"?

I forgot all about that little detour until six years later when my husband and I chose that church to be ours. After we officially joined, we were given a directory with names and pictures of all the members of the congregation and told it was quite old, but they would be doing another soon.

As I flipped through the pages, I stopped at one photo of the sanctuary full of people. I could not believe what I saw.

There in the fourth pew from the front, in the midst of people with the joy of the spirit in their expressions, was Heather and me. As for my image, that broken and disappointed version of myself that sat stiffly among strangers, was so different than the happy, at-peace person who was looking at the photo.

I was later baptized in that church.

I wanted my cleansing to be right there in that same sanctuary. I needed to leave behind the ghost of that girl I used to be and embrace my new and wonderful life.

As I write this chapter, my husband and I are close to celebrating our twenty-seventh wedding anniversary. I had always said I'd have my first real wedding at our tenth then moved it out to our twentieth. I wanted to know what it felt like to wear a wedding gown, to say our vows in church. With paying for college educations, houses, and many other things, we never put aside a budget for that wedding.

But I no longer care. What my Ben and I have is what some only dream of—a true partnership of love and loyalty. He has never raised his hand to me, and we've never had a screaming match or called each other names that can't be taken back.

We have so many blessing in our life, with our five grandchildren and three bonus-grands being at the very top of the list. I always knew that my Ben would be the world's best Papa, and he is that and more.

I won't say everything is perfect because no relationship is. We've been through some hard times. Remember SARS? We were there in China when it started and would later consider it our "practice pandemic."

We were in Thailand during the deadliest tsunami in history that killed more than two hundred thousand people. Thankfully we were on the opposite side of the most affected areas, though we had just been to Phuket and Phi Phi Islands not long before they were nearly wiped out.

During another ordeal in China, Ben came down with a serious illness that quickly got out of control. Three hospitals, a ton of morphine, and pleadings from him to *just let him die*, the company made plans to evacuate us out of China on a private medical jet.

The Chinese didn't want to let him go because they were using him (and his agony) as a mysterious-illness teaching moment. The team that came in to grab him were Cantonese, and they quickly transferred him from the hospital bed to the wheeled stretcher, then the two groups proceeded to have a tug-of-war with my husband.

Literally.

Finally, we were able to break free of the Chinese and got him out of there, into the ambulance, and then conquered a ride from hell to the airport.

To say it was terrifying is putting it mildly. I thought Ben was going to die.

They delivered us to Happy Valley Sanatorium in China where a surgeon waited for us in the middle of the night, the operating room set up to take Ben's leg.

I begged for more time before amputating, and miraculously, within twenty-four hours, they found the right drug to get his staph infection and necrotizing fasciitis (flesh-eating disease) under control. Ben still spent nearly a month as a patient there while they performed excruciating daily wound cleaning, wound packing, and then rehabilitation to get him back on his feet.

Later, we would get a second wind of dealing with a pandemic when Ben was one of the first to be ill in the Covid crisis and nearly lost his life. The team of doctors told us that if we'd have waited one more day to come to the hospital, they would've been discussing morbidity rates with us. Unfortunately, no one yet knew what Covid was or how it would affect so many people.

Yes, with tragedies, illnesses, and freaky natural disasters, we can never call our life together boring. Hardest of all for me has been the constant struggle I've gone through with my daughter, Heather. I love her so much, and it kills me to see her wasting her youth on bad choices. It's been a roller coaster of a life with her, though at the time of writing this I'm happy to say that she's beginning to get things together and has decided to spend more time with her children.

That's the thing, though. It's her choice. I can try to

help, and I have, but at the end of the day, all I can do is let her know that as long as I'm still on this Earth, she will have someone who loves every hair on her head. I won't enable her like I used to do, but I will pray for her. And who knows, one day she may read this book and be a different kind of person. A healthy one with a life of joy. I do think she's doing better each day, and I'll keep hoping and praying for it to continue.

Ben and I get through it all together. He is my rock and my best friend, and he says the same thing about me. I know we are each other's biggest cheerleaders and have helped one another reach the successes in our careers that we have.

I thank the Lord for my two beautiful daughters, five biological grandchildren, and three bonus grands. We live in a house we planned from the ground up and enjoy evening cruising on the lake—quiet ones in our alone time and embracing the organized chaos when the kids come.

God also blessed me with the ability to hone my writing skills and wrangle all my life's experiences into novels that bring out emotion in the readers. I often say I'm ready to retire my keyboard, that it takes too many hours to do what I do. Then I take some time off and am just dying to get back to creating my stories. I can't *not* tell them, or they will take over my brain and drive me round the bend.

I love the work I get to do with dog rescue, and Ben finally just accepts it. When he discovered I'd been going into a meth-infested neighborhood alone to care for a dog on a chain, he decided that to keep me from sneaking around, he'd better just agree to go with me.

On that occasion, he went to work, getting a warm igloo doghouse and drilling it to a pallet so the dog could be out of the mud. With help from my Krew—my online networks of my most-trusted peeps—we brought over the doghouse and toys, plus food and gift cards for the pack dad who was struggling in life.

Just last night, the temperatures were supposed to drop here, so we delivered straw and chew bones to six different dogs on two properties. Ben has embraced my crazy, I like to tell him. I love that we have so many laughs together.

He's a good, good man.

I have been so blessed, y'all.

There is still hard stuff, though.

As many of you know, sometimes the trials of your life can bring distance between you and your family members. With as much as my siblings and I went through as kids, and going our separate ways as such young adults, there really isn't a close relationship between us to speak of. Not like I dream of sometimes.

A few weeks ago, someone asked me what my little sister's favorite color is. I had no idea. How can I not know the favorite color of the sister I once protected, put her hair up in pigtails, and comforted when she was sad?

That made me realize that I don't know my brother's favorite color either. Or what he likes to eat. Or watch on television. Or even his dog's name.

How is that possible? He was always my big brother, and for fifteen years, we were siblings under the same roof. Yet because of his own life trauma, he has chosen to isolate himself from the world, including most of his family, and I've respected his choices.

Respected them, though they make me sad.

I think we all love each other, but we have so many demons, and we share a lot of trauma that stands between us, each of us dealing with it in our own stubborn way.

There is also a chasm between my mother and me.

That is the one that hurts me the deepest. I suppose maybe for years I didn't admit that I felt she should hold some of the blame for the tumultuous childhood we had. She has really never known how to relate to me. Someone who knows her better than she knows herself told me that it's because my mom has always been a soldier-like person. Just do the hard stuff. Get it done. No fluff.

With me, she had a daughter who, once she signed off on my first marriage license, was determined not to come back or ask her for help. Then when I finally did, she was embroiled in her own drama and couldn't be there for me like I wanted her to.

I had to figure it all out myself.

The exact way that she did when she got married at the young age of fifteen.

Ironically, we are more alike than either of us would like to admit.

When I turned fifty, I wrote her a long letter. In it, I confessed everything I'd been holding on to and forgave her for it, whether she had known I felt that way or not.

Then I privately acknowledged that for my mom, a young mother of four kids at the age of only twenty-five, she did the best she could while trying to keep up with my dad's wanderlust and dragging us all over the country. In those early years, he was a drinker and not the easiest husband or father. If not anything else, my mom always tried to keep her children safe. She worked so very hard, and despite the raging wars between them, my parents kept us together under one roof. It's pretty spectacular that somehow both her and my father always made it work.

Until it didn't.

I never blamed my mom for wanting her freedom when she divorced my dad. Their marriage was toxic at a level that was unhealthy for all involved. My mom never got to be her own person, and at the age of thirty-three, she decided it was time.

What happened in the aftermath was not all her fault.

I know that now. I acknowledge that.

And I've moved on.

My father turned seventy years old recently, and we decided to rent a house in the mountains then try really hard to get all his kids to come.

Because of Covid, we had to cancel.

Over the years, my dad has acknowledged his wrongs and tried to make up for them. In my adult life, he's been a great father. He's a good man, a very hard worker, and would give you the shirt off his back if he thought you really needed it. He also has not had a drink of alcohol in more than thirty years and even apologized to my mom for all the ways he ever hurt her, which are plentiful.

They are both remarried now, but some of her scars will never heal, and that's her choice whether to forgive or not. For me, I'll always choose to let things go. Not because I think I'm some sort of saint but because letting go of that anger and resentment is what God wants us to do and is also healing for myself.

After the trip was canceled, Dad said all he wanted was for his kids to take him to Oklahoma to see his father's grave for one last time. I'm not a miracle maker, so rounding them all up for something wasn't going to happen. But he's never really asked for anything, so Ben and I decided to take him. We rented an RV so that we could make a road trip out of it.

The trip that was planned for him became a journey of healing for me that was totally unexpected. Our first big stop was Arkansas City, Kansas—or Ark City, as it is known.

The only thing the small town is famous for is that it was the rendezvous point of the settlers who, back in 1893, were jockeying for a valuable piece of the Cherokee Strip Land Run, which was one of the largest land runs in the history of the United States. Many people waited for the event, living in tents and wagons in Boomer camps, some nearly starved as they hoped to have a piece of the land. Unfortunately, from what I've read, it sounds to me like, once again, the Cherokee Indians were treated unfairly in this "forced sale" of six million acres and more than forty thousand homesteads.

As the story is told, more than one hundred thousand settlers lined up in covered wagons, oxcarts, and on bicycles, racehorses, and even Indian ponies, waiting for the go. Despite infantry and calvary troops stationed strategically, many people were still able to sneak in before the first pistol shots were fired to start the run, in order to secure (steal) some of the best locations.

I can only imagine the generations of rich families in the area who are affluent only because of their ancestors' underhanded acts that resulted in the catalyst to building wealth.

The town still isn't much to look at and definitely nothing to brag about, but for the first time, I saw the homes my parents each grew up in, the window my mom would sneak out of, the spots they would meet to see each other. I imagined my mom at the age of fourteen, watching for my dad to come and him welcoming her into his arms then sneaking off into the night.

I wondered, what were her dreams back then? What was she like?

My mother had four older brothers and a twin brother. She is so tough that it's hard for me to imagine her as the only girl and baby of the family, though I suppose that is what made her tough.

Dad told me of the night they ran away together, stealing one of my grandpa's cars, and how it broke down, and they had to come home. I knocked on that door of my mom's old house and explained to the woman who answered that my mom grew up there. I asked if I could just step in and look.

What a gift she gave me by allowing me into the foyer. The house is very old and a bit rundown, but I'd like to call it well-loved. The grand staircase was the first thing that greeted me. I remember my dad telling me of when my mom's brother came home from the navy, and Dad was introduced as the boy she'd run away with and who was going to marry her.

"Damn right he is," was the reply from my gruff uncle. I'm sure if he hadn't have come home to make sure it happened, her other brothers would've done so.

Straight ahead was the kitchen where I quickly imagined my beloved grandma cooking in there for her big family. I thought of my mom around the table with her brothers, eating before she headed upstairs for homework or for pining for my dad.

To my left were double doors that led to the library or living room. I saw an old armchair in there and could see my grandfather—who I only remembered from photos—sitting there having a smoke after a long day. Or playing poker with his friends, as he was known to do.

Did he ever imagine the long line of descendants he would start?

My dad took me to the courthouse where my maternal grandmother marched them up the steps to get married after finding out they were sleeping together. Coincidentally, it was in Kay County, Oklahoma—another surprise that Dad said he'd never noticed.

We drove by little places they rented when they were married, some just one-room apartments where they survived on next to nothing with their tiny family. At one house that set up high, he showed me where my mom rolled him down the hill after he came home drunk after leaving her there alone with three babies to tend.

I could see her doing that. Her temper is legendary and still a force to be reckoned with.

What really struck me was that she was so young. She

could've dumped her kids on someone else and joined my dad. Or even left us home alone.

That was not her way. She was the epitome of a mother bear, putting her own wants and dreams aside in the interest of doing the right thing for her kids.

Now that Dad was opening up about their lives for the first time, I wanted to know everything he could tell me.

Where did he work? How did they make it?

My thirst for details was all-consuming.

We drove by a place that used to be a small-town grocery where Dad worked, clearing out the upstairs from all the hoarding the owner had done over the years. His payment was a set of old Jenny Lind high chairs.

I found it astonishing that my dad of only twenty years old, with three kids and a wife, put in the blood, sweat, and tears just so that my twin sister and I could have new-to-us high chairs. For so many years, I felt like we were always such a burden to them both. The stories from him of the things he and my mom did when we (and they) were so young was very eye-opening and showed me that yes, we were loved.

Not with words or touches of affection but with gestures to show they cared.

Even at my mom's young age, she always cooked for all of us. I remember at only six and seven years old when we lived at the motel, going to school with a belly full of warm oatmeal topped with sprinkles of sugar. We didn't have fancy foods, but we had enough. That was her way of showing her love.

I saw the bar that my dad went to the night my brother was born. I imagined him as a young man of only seventeen, a new proud father who had no idea what was in store for his life. In all of the places my dad showed me from their early years, he only praised my mom—acknowledging what a wonderful and protective young mother she was. He admitted to being a horrible husband to her for a long time, allowing his own lack of self-worth to lead him wrong and make him hurt my mom emotionally. He said she was a good woman and had stood by him through it all, just so that we could stay a family.

Seeing everything as an adult made me really feel for the young people who were my parents. I realized my mom was just like me when I jumped into adulthood too soon. She just wanted to prove to everyone she could do it, even if it killed her. She was a child herself when she became a mother, but she gave everything up to be who we needed her to be. As imperfect as she was, she tried with all she had.

Simply put, finally I saw her humanity and realized that my expectations were not truly a realistic standard for where my parents came from and who they were.

Before this trip, I had not really seen them as children or as young, married teenagers, nor did I acknowledge that the hardships of my childhood paled in comparison to those of theirs. Looking at who they are now makes me feel so very proud of all they have accomplished through their hard work, ethics, and the values that were instilled in them from their own families.

Leaving behind their hometown, we headed to a cemetery in Perkins, Oklahoma.

The visit to my grandfather's grave was somber but also very satisfying.

I wrote a book a few years back called *True to Me*. It involved a character who took a DNA test to try to find her biological family. As research for the process, I took one too.

When my results came back, I had a conversation with my dad about it.

"What did it show?" he asked.

"Well, first of all, Mom isn't part Cherokee as she always thought," I said. "We don't have a drop of Indian blood in us."

"What else?"

"Just a lot of Bateson cousins and people I don't know." Remember, we grew up all over the country, and I can't say I knew any relatives that well, other than my grandmother.

He was quiet for a minute.

"What do you mean, a lot of Batesons?"

"There are a lot of your relatives listed," I said. "Many of mom's too."

"Does that mean that without a doubt you have Bateson blood?"

"Yes," I answered, confused.

He was quiet again.

Then he spoke. "You've just confirmed something for me that I've wanted to know all my life."

"What do you mean, Dad?"

I knew he didn't have my grandpa's last name, but I never knew the details why. It just wasn't talked about, and I felt it was too sensitive a subject to ask.

He explained to me that his dad couldn't marry my grandmother. And when my dad was born, she didn't give him his father's name. Most of the Batesons didn't acknowledge my dad as one of them. A few did, but Dad always felt like an outsider, even though his dad was good to him and was a loving father.

When my dad was only fifteen, his father died.

There had been rumors that my dad wasn't really a Bateson, and back in those days, it was like wearing a scarlet letter. The doubt of others put a seed of worry in his child's heart that followed him for his entire life. To even think of the pain he hid in his attempt to appear fearless and undaunted makes me sad.

What irony that my ambition to be more than my humble beginnings led to the best gift I could ever give my dad, which was the truth of who he is, that the man he loved desperately is indeed his biological father.

My grandfather.

I don't know what my dad said at the grave because Ben and I gave him privacy, but there were a lot of tears. I think, and I hope dearly, that he finally found peace in his identity.

It was surreal for me to walk around the cemetery and see the stones of so many family members who I didn't know existed. At one woman's grave, my dad commented that he had gone to her house for Sunday lunches when he was a kid. To me, that was an enthralling piece of history.

Speaking of history, my grandfather is laid to rest only about twenty feet from the famed Pistol Pete of the old west. His real name was Frank Eaton, and he was known to have grown up a master marksman who went out to avenge his father's death at the hands of six former Confederates. He learned to shoot at age fifteen at a calvary fort and beat out all the marksmen to earn him his nickname and was rumored to be "the fastest gun in Indian territory". He supposedly served as a U.S. deputy marshal and later a sheriff. When we left the grave, we visited the small museum of Pistol Pete, and I later found out that my second cousin used to be great friends with the man and one time had picked up a gun in front of Pistol Pete only to be reprimanded by him.

"If you gonna aim that gun at someone, you'd better be prepared to shoot it," Pete told my cousin, Gary Bateson.

Pistol Pete died at age ninety-seven with nine children and many great grandchildren to his name. My cousin, rest his soul, died of Covid a few months after telling me that story.

After we visited my grandfather's grave in Oklahoma, we stayed in Kansas one more night. The next morning on our way out, we went by the last place I knew my maternal grandmother to live. It's a seven-floor senior living building, and it held many memories for me. I went up the elevator just like we always did on our occasional visits to her from our many places we lived.

I stood in front of the window we'd peek in through, and I cried, wishing that once again she would peek out, and her face would fill with such joy as she rushed to let us in. A part of me wanted to knock on the door and ask the resident if I could come in and try to feel my grandmother there, but the other part knew that there was no way possible that the apartment would look nearly as cozy and full without all my grandma's crafty projects and her love. I decided to keep the memory of what it used to be, instead of what it became after she was gone.

My grandmother always told me I was special. I'm sure she told all her grandchildren that, and I didn't believe it anyway, but she gave me hope that it could be true. She predicted that I wouldn't always be the traumatized young woman I was when I saw her last—hiding from my abusive ex—and that God had a purpose laid out for me.

Several years ago, when my interest in signs from the other side was at its highest, I asked my grandmother for a sign that she was around and knew that I had finally made a better life for myself. A few nights later, I was sitting up in bed, reading my Kindle.

Ben was asleep beside me, but he woke when he heard me gasp.

A tiny white feather had floated gently down from the ceiling and landed right on the Kindle where I was reading. We didn't have birds. Or any other explanation for why a feather would be in our house, much less come down from the ceiling.

It was a surreal moment, and I immediately felt my grandmother's presence.

Back in Kansas, walking around the place she lived

her last years and handed down love to every one of her grandchildren, I was filled with such regret that I didn't find a way to visit her after I married, to allow her to see the man who would rescue my heart.

I asked for a sign in the building. *Speak to me, Grandma*, I begged.

There was nothing inside, and I went out the door feeling sad. Then I looked at my feet as I took the path toward the RV. Stuck in the gravel there, and the only adornment, was a metal sunflower.

My mother likes for the sunflower to represent her.

Could my grandmother be sending me a sign that she wanted me to try to bridge that gap between myself and her only daughter?

That was definitely something to think on.

The next morning, we headed to Nebraska. Just before we arrived, I made a decision to try to meet with Tracy's mom. I got her address from her daughter through Facebook, and we pulled up in the big RV.

So very nervous, with my heart pounding, I walked up to her door and knocked.

She wasn't home.

We were leaving that town immediately, to be able to make our schedule and have the RV back on time. I was never going to have another chance. Dad was watching through the window of the RV. He knew how much I needed this reunion.

I turned to leave, and as I was walking back to the RV, Tracy's mom, Janet, pulled into the driveway. We hadn't seen each other for thirty-five years, but I recognized her immediately. She looked the same to me. That same engaging smile.

I met her just behind the car, and when she stepped out, she looked puzzled. And a little wary. She had a huge RV sitting in front of her house and a stranger in her driveway. Of course she wondered what the heck was going on.

I was so nervous. Would it hurt her to see me? Bring her more pain?

I had to take the chance.

"Remember me?" I asked, knowing there was no way she'd know who I was.

Janet doesn't have online profiles in any social network platforms. I was ten years old when I saw her last.

She stared at me for just a second longer then said my name softly, as though she couldn't believe it.

I nodded, and we fell into each other's arms, hugging like there was no tomorrow.

Dad and Ben joined us, and we all chatted outside for a few minutes.

Janet was incredulous that I was actually there, just dropping in from so far away and without notice. I told her that her eldest daughter had given me the address.

Then I asked Dad and Ben if they'd give us some time alone.

She and I sat down on the porch steps, and she took my hand. A big cat crawled up between us too. That cat gave me some courage. I swear it did.

There on that cold porch in Nebraska, I told Janet every detail of what happened that horrific afternoon that she lost her daughter. As I talked, I cried from a place of guilt and sorrow, so deep in my soul that it felt endless.

When I stopped for a breath, Janet told me something that I did not know. Two weeks before the accident, Tracy overheard her parents talking about organ donation. At only eleven years old, she told them she wanted to be an organ donor.

Janet took note of her daughter's wishes, though she never thought she'd be the one to give that answer to fulfill them.

The day of the accident, the mother of one of our other

friends approached the scene. She was an RN, and she alone kept Tracy alive until the ambulance crew arrived and took over. That in itself was a miracle that she happened by at the exact right moment out on that country highway, but for me to know that somewhere in the world someone is walking around with Tracy's beautiful eyes (and other organs) is a balm to my soul.

The only thing they couldn't save was her brain because the impact of the damage couldn't be reversed.

Janet also spoke softly and confessed that in the months after the accident, she felt so much guilt that she didn't know how she'd get through it. When Janet had given Tracy permission to come with us that day, she was unaware that it was an unsupervised home, or she wouldn't have been in that spot at that moment.

She blamed herself.

But finally, God gave her a vision of Tracy in Heaven, surrounded by a lot of children, with one on her hip. Tracy was always infatuated with kids and they with her. The vision was so vivid and real that it helped Janet find the peace she needed to go on and raise her remaining children.

I cried again, for her pain and for mine. I asked her if she could ever really forgive me, that not a day had gone by that I have not thought of Tracy. That every time I approach a busy highway or street on foot, I feel fear in my heart. That with every passing ambulance, I relive that day and wish they could've gotten to her sooner. That I've always feared one of my children would be taken the same way, for some sort of twisted justice.

As I talked, I was once again that child, crying to her and saying I'm sorry.

I'm so, so sorry. Sorry, sorry, sorry.

Please forgive me.

With her arms wrapped tightly around me, she said what I'd needed to hear for decades.

"Yes, you are forgiven."

She didn't think I had anything to be forgiven for, but she knew I needed to hear those words. Then she asked me to forgive her, for she had no idea of the post-traumatic pain my siblings and I carried for so long. All she knew was that pretty soon after, we'd up and moved.

I think we both needed that day more than we knew.

Dad took a photo of us together, memorializing that moment of freedom for me. I sent Janet a copy of it for Christmas, engraved with a scripture of forgiveness, the one thing that neither of us should've needed to ask for but both of us wanted.

We left Janet and then did a tour around the last town we'd lived in Nebraska, a few hours from there. I had missed Taco John for years, and we stopped there, and I ran in and got some, then we ate it in the RV. It did not live up to my memory. I guess my taste buds have matured too.

Then Dad took me out of town to where we lived in the farmhouse. It was one of the places I needed to see, and my anticipation was mixed with trepidation and years of built-up anxiety. But when we got near enough to see, we realized there was nothing there but a big, flat field.

How could it be gone? The main house and our cute little rental home? The barn and Sam's pen. The many haystack castles I hid in and read my books. And why would someone raze it to the ground? Obviously, I knew there wasn't any way that Miss Charlotte could still be living, but I think something in me hoped it was true anyway. But to not even get to see her home where she offered us such good baked things? Where we felt the love of a grandparent that being so far from our hometown had us craving?

I felt like something was stolen from me.

I also remembered the many times I walked Sam

around there. The afternoons we played with barn kittens and the field mice in the kitchen.

I wished so badly it was still standing.

The old haunted house across the way was gone too. It was our goal that terrible afternoon, and I was glad not to lay eyes on it. We tried to find the place on the highway where I knelt next to Tracy, begging her to get up, but I suppose God didn't want to leave me with that memory because without the landmarks I'd known, we couldn't find it.

Finally, ready for the moment that had been haunting me for more than three decades, I said my goodbye to Tracy's ghost, somewhere in the vicinity of where I last saw her alive. I can honestly say that for the first time, I no longer felt like that traumatized girl who stood on the side of the road and watched a horrific scene unfold.

Ben held my hand, and we somberly moved on.

Next, we drove over the actual train tracks where my siblings and I were almost hit by a train in the car of a mom who was carpooling that morning. I had forgotten about it until we approached the crossing and instantly remembered. Down a bit more on that gravel road, we found the little school, Alfalfa Center.

It's now a private home, but there were memories there too. Some fond, especially of the home-cooked meals that would send aromas up into the classrooms midmorning, taunting us and making us too hungry to concentrate. I thought about gathering around the big piano for music class. I loved to sing, and one song we sang a lot there was "Orion is Arising" by Jim Zimmerman. I haven't heard it since 1980 or so, but I still remember every word.

I loved that class and the thundering piano. But there was hard stuff too. A teacher there was known for her overuse of her talon-like nails on the back of our necks as she stood behind us, unhappy with our work or talking in class. After she left a few marks on us, my mom had *a talk* with her, and there were no more talon marks on her kids after that. My mom was scary when you made her mad.

Actually, she still is.

Onward bound, we headed to the tiny town of Odessa, which, like Kearney, was a part of Buffalo County. Before it became a county, huge herds of buffalo grazed there, and later, it was known for the two transportation lines that ran through.

The Mormon Trail and the Pacific Railroad.

It was also land upon which a fierce war was waged between the Sioux and the Cheyenne tribes, forcing settlers out for a time until the fighting eased, and they came back. The area has a long history of severe blizzards, and most interestingly was part of the massive acres of lands demolished by a wave of grasshoppers back in the 1870s.

Can you imagine the devastation of toiling on your land day in and day out, only to lose all your crops to a scene that appears to have come straight out of the pages of the Bible? I read up on the history of Odessa, and it's a captivating tale of sod houses, prairie fires, and excursions up and down the Platte River.

When we moved there in the mid-seventies, Odessa was a tiny run-down town. When I visited again as an adult, it felt even tinier and more run-down. Our elementary school, where my favorite teacher in the whole world taught, is now a furniture store.

Brenda Martin.

I thought of her and was filled with sadness. She was beautiful, and I can still picture her amazing smile. She was loving and kind and made us want to learn, just to please her. I remember a day that she and her husband came out to the motel with brand-new winter coats for my siblings and me. She also climbed up on the tall bars with me when I was too frightened to come down by myself, and she gently coached me to the ground.

Her life ended in a tragic suicide. She died in her car parked in her garage, overcome by fumes. I let that thought go as I asked Dad to please find my church.

Not just any church.

But the church where my faith began.

I was so thankful that the tiny one-room building was still standing. It's drastically run-down and abandoned, but the good memories came flooding back with the sight of the front door. Through the bare trees, I could see the old outhouse and remembered running around out there with other kids, my brother guarding the door when my sister and I had to use the scary, dark hole.

In front of the church again, I stood back and took a photo. With the sun setting behind it, casting a beautiful glow on the little building, I let out a deep breath of affection for the place that I first found my faith. I marveled at how far from there I'd gone, but in essence, how far I have come.

When we left there, I was spent.

We made a dash for Nashville and got into a campground late. The next morning, my dad surprised us with a detour to Cocke County and the courthouse where Ben and I got married. We hadn't seen it in nearly thirty years, so it was a special way to end the road trip.

One of the biggest blessings of the entire trip was spending that time with my dad. We talked, laughed, and he told me lots of stories from his life that I'd never heard. I also appreciate that, by actually seeing some of the places I've been and lived, I was able to dredge up more good memories than I knew I had. I realized again that while our lives were humble, we had so much more than many had, and my parents had done the best that they knew how.

I came home a new person. I really did. All my life

I've lamented that I don't really have a home. Or roots. When people talk about going back to their hometown, I apply it to my life, and I don't know where that would be. Or at least, I didn't. Many people consider home to be where they started and where they can still find family. I think that what my life, and the last road trip, has taught me is that home can be wherever you feel fulfilled and at peace. A turtle carries its home on its back, but I choose to carry mine in my heart. I don't need to feel the soil sifted between my fingers because I've built memories that are untouchable.

In closing, let's get back to the point of this book and why I wrote it.

Do dogs go to Heaven?

I don't plan to convince you or anyone else that dogs and other animals will be in Heaven. I do not wish to argue with skeptics. I don't have any background in theology or a direct connection to talk to spirits—I'm not even sure anyone does—or a single credential that would make me a quotable, reliable source.

I am simply a writer who loves dogs and someone who has always poured out her feelings using the written word. I have also always had an unquenchable thirst to know more about otherworldly things. Perhaps that is because it is rumored that my great-grandmother was born with a caul—or what some call born with a veil over her face. While some consider it a normal part of birth for some babies, others believe those who have it are touched with something special. Could it be that somehow my ancestor and I are attached in a way that keeps me asking questions and trying to find answers? Possibly, though I know that most of them will only become clear when it is my time to take my last journey.

If you have made it this far, I want to thank you for joining me on the road trip of my life. Truth be told, I am not the person that I once was, and I am not the person I want to be. I am somewhere in the middle and will keep striving to be better. I've learned that healing from a hypervigilant childhood is about embracing the freedom to tend to my boundaries and emotional needs now, as an adult. I've also decided that I need to stop keeping secrets. I want to be heard, not fixed. I've realized that things that happened in my past were a bigger deal than I was allowed to think they were. Or at least, to me they were.

As I look back on everything and think how I've gone through the fires, mostly unscathed, I know I was not alone.

And neither are you.

He was there and is there, right beside you.

If you have never accepted that gift, I hope you do.

About the animals, it is up to you alone to decide if you believe you will see your beloved pets when it's your time to leave your earthly existence. In the next chapters, I've included some of my research as it pertains to biblical proof. You can read it or skip it, but as for me and my house, or the Bratt Pack, as they have come to be known, I have already decided that I am absolutely positive that all (my) dogs go to Heaven.

Illustration by Ken Robinson of Express Portraits:
Grandpa Oliver and Hazel Bea,
Connected by a Love for Me.

24

DO DOGS HAVE SOULS?

One argument that continues to rage across the world today is that animals cannot go to Heaven because they do not have souls. Let's talk about that. An interesting fact that I discovered in my research is that the word animal is derived from the Latin word *anima,* which means "soul." In the creation story, the Hebrew word *nephesh* translates to "soul" and means life. In Genesis, it is used equally for mankind, as well as creatures of the air, sea, and land (Genesis 1:20, 1:24, 2:7).

In 1990, Pope John Paul II stated, "also the animals possess a soul and men must love and feel solidarity with smaller brethren." Later he said that animals are "as near to God as men are."

In Ecclesiastes 3:19, it speaks of men and beasts all having "one spirit. "

Obviously, the soul of a human is more advanced than the soul of an animal, and there is a clear difference in the body of humans vs. animals and all their anatomy. However, like humans, animals are able to display intentional communication, compassion, loyalty, sorrow, and joy.

Many animals understand and adhere to the pack mentality—or in human terms, family structure. And like humans, animals have different personalities and characteristics from one creature to the other.

I believe that our soul is what gives humans their personality. Therefore, if animals have personalities that differentiate, then they indeed have a soul as we do.

Mitch Albom, author of the New York Times bestselling books, *The Five People You Meet in Heaven*, and *Tuesdays with Morrie*, says, "dogs are not human in biology, but their love, devotion, affection, and protection are certainly characteristics of a living, caring personality presence. And if you believe in God, you surely see a divine touch in their creation."

Let's take a look at this scripture in Revelations. "And every creature which is in Heaven, and on the earth, and under the earth, and such as are in the sea, and all that are in them, heard I saying, Blessing, and honor, and glory, and power, be unto him that sitteth upon the throne, and unto the Lamb for ever and ever."

First, it says, "every creature which is in heaven."

"Creature" is the all-embracing word in the Bible for animals that "have breath." And I think we can all agree that dogs are animals that have breath. Sometimes very atrocious breath, you might add. Then the scripture says, "which is in heaven," but in the next line, it says, "and on the earth," then goes on to include those under earth, and *in the sea*. Sounds to me like that covers all of them no matter where they are, right?

Right.

The scripture ends with, "they are heard giving praise to God," just as the book of John predicted would happen one day.

Amen to that, y'all.

25

WATCH OUT FOR THAT GHOST

Heartwarming stories of people connecting with their beloved, departed dogs are wonderful, but for some of us, we long to know more. How is it possible? Are they ghosts? A figment of our imagination? From all of my research over the last few years that first involved humans giving messages from beyond the grave and then expanded to dogs, there is one key word that kept cropping up over and over.

Energy.

Not ghosts. Well, I guess that can be argued too. Not that I'm saying ghosts don't exist. Or do exist. That's a subject for a different book. For this one, I'd rather go with a real explanation that has a bit of footing in logic.

Niels Bohr, a Danish physicist who specializes in understanding atomic structure and quantum theory and has won a Nobel Prize, has this to say, "If quantum mechanics hasn't profoundly shocked you, you haven't understood it yet. Everything we call real is made of things that cannot be regarded as real."

I'm not going to get into a scientific explanation or debate because, honestly, I'm not that smart. Though I like to have facts to back up anything I read, and I do extensive research, I could never stand up against a proven scholar, and really, some things will never be confirmed beyond a reasonable doubt.

That's called faith, if you've forgotten.

However, I can attest that I've read several books by skeptics with scientific minds who are now, after specific experiences, believers that life is not over at death.

I have a practical personality, and though I love a good story that makes me cry happy tears, I relish the accounts from the really smart cookies, like doctors and scientists. For it is those types of skeptic-turned-believers who I feel lend a more scientifically based opinion that can bring some sense of comfort to my curious mind.

Take, for example, Dr. Eben Alexander, a neurosurgeon considered highly rational and of impeccable credentials who has operated on thousands of brains. Through most of his career, he considered anything supernatural that happened with the soul, like near-death experiences, to be the result of brain chemistry, merely fantasies created by brains under stress.

When Eben became ill with a bacterial infection, the part of his brain that is connected to his consciousness completely shut down. Conscious experience wasn't scientifically possible in his vegetative state.

In the coma he slipped into, Eben experienced a world beyond his imagination and everything that he had ever been taught about science and the universe. When he emerged from the coma and miraculously recovered, his experiences made him a believer that death is not the end of a human's existence but only a transition. You can find out more about his story in his book *Proof of Heaven* and, most interestingly, read why he argues against the ability of the brain to create what he experienced.

Reading his story, among others, made me realize that I believe that something does indeed come after death for humans. It's a reunion with the God who created you and me, in a place that He is making ready. And because I believe that is what happens to humans, then I wondered if it could also be possible for animals.

Obviously, I decided yes, it is possible.

That doesn't mean I believed immediately that animals could somehow let us know they are near after they have departed. It would take much more research for me to figure out my stance on that because I wanted to know how it could be possible.

So, here's what all of my curiosity has led me to.

Energy, again.

Throughout the universe, a formless energy is invisible but is there. Like a whisper in the wind, we can sometimes feel it, though there is no proof of it. It's impossible to destroy energy, but rumor has it that it can be transformed, into something or someone, from one point to another. Have you ever noticed when you are around someone that has a very loud and energetic personality that after a while, you feel drained? That person has a very strong energy, which can be good or bad, depending on how they rein it in or use it. Those overpowering energies can also be a detriment to sensitive people who do better around a more low-key energy source.

It is my belief that we all share a combined energy that is connected to our Lord and savior, and that energy plays a vital role in births, deaths, and the lessons we are to learn during our time here on Earth.

Think about the movie *Ghost*, with Patrick Swayze. His love interest thinks she can feel him, and Patrick's spirit is struggling so hard to figure out how to pull all his energy together from the other side to give her a sign that yes, he is there. Of course, that movie is fiction, but I still think that it's a very good depiction of how our loved ones, or departed pets, try to harness their energy to comfort us from the other side.

In the book *The Amazing Afterlife of Animals*, Karen A. Anderson is a self-proclaimed afterlife expert and animal communicator. She writes an interesting description of where the other side is. She says it's not some far away universe, and that it is all around us. In her words, the other side is where an animal's energy exists after their physical body dies, and they can travel between the other dimension (I call Heaven or Eternity) and Earth. Karen says the animals have communicated to her that, "the other side is a comfortable, loving, joyous space that encompasses the same areas they enjoyed in physical form."

Scientists agree that we are made up of energy and matter. I believe that when you combine energy with the most powerful gift God ever gave us—love—then miracles can happen. If a spirit is strong enough, and not all animals are because they vibrate at lower frequencies than humans do, they are able to communicate from the other side.

If you are open to receiving such gifts of supernatural love, you will sense it, hear it, or feel it. Y'all, love doesn't die.

Let me say that again for those in the back row.

LOVE. DOESN'T. DIE.

26

DREAMING OF YOUR DOG

M any grieving pet owners have reported that their dogs (or cats) came to them in a dream, but does this mean it was really the spirit of their pet? To answer that, you must first determine if it was a dream or a visitation. Most of us have dreams, and some of them can be quite creative or fantastical. I myself have always had very vivid dreams, as well as have suffered from night terrors all of my life in which I see people who are not really there. After my tumultuous first marriage and the trauma I went through with physical abuse, threats, and stalking, my night terrors were at their worst.

The recurring one was of a silent and threatening figure chasing me down. I'm running, running, and trying to stay just a finger's breadth away from him. It's always up and down stairs, around hallways, into the woods, or many other scenarios, but the terror and foreboding feelings are visceral, and I wake up just before he catches me, usually perspiring and exhausted from the running. One particular night, just after I married Ben, I was still having the dreams, and during the night terror, I jumped out of bed and started running.

In the night terror, I was going straight down a long corridor.

However, in my actual home, I ran straight out of the bedroom and into the kitchen, slamming my face into the refrigerator and nearly knocking myself out. Too bad I didn't see that fridge in my dream so I could make a detour, right?

Unfortunately, at the time, I was wearing adult braces on my teeth, and after the impact, the inside of my lip resembled ground meat. How would you like to go in and explain to your orthodontist that you got in a fight with a side-by-side?

I'm happy to report that once I felt loved and protected by my husband (we are now in year twenty-seven of a wonderful marriage) that those specific night terrors stopped. Our brains are wired for human connection and relationships, and we aren't meant to be alone with our painful memories and stress. My Ben knows that the terrible dreams or uncomfortable feelings I have sometimes doesn't mean that something is wrong with me, it just means I'm human. He gives me the emotional safety to feel them, then put them away.

The only time I have night terrors now are when I'm overly exhausted or I have to sleep in a strange place. I remember our first night in Shanghai, they put us up in the Grand Hyatt hotel, which has eighty-seven floors. Our room was on the twenty-first floor, which was still too high for me because I'm terrified of heights. However, we were exhausted from the thirty hours it took for us to get there, so we made do. (This was before there were direct flights, and we had to switch planes twice.)

The bed they gave us in the room was so tiny that my Ben and I barely fit on it. Only our youngest was with us, so we made her a soft place to sleep on the floor.

I sat up in bed, looking wide-awake and petrified.

"Amanda's on the balcony!" I screamed.

Ben jumped out of bed, yanked open the drapes, then turned back and screamed.

"There ain't no flipping balcony!" (His words may have been a bit more colorful.)

He just about had a heart attack before he realized I was having a night terror, and his little girl was fast asleep on the floor.

Okay, that was not a dream. Nor a visitation.

It was a night terror.

All that to say is if your pet is coming to you, and it is not a fictional dream, it is a visitation and will be extremely detailed. It should leave you with a feeling of peace and/or as though you were given a message. In some accounts of visitations, they were so real that once awakened, the person raced around their home looking for their pet or evidence it had been there.

In closing, anyone can ask their pet to visit them in their dreams. If the pet has banked up enough energy to make it happen—or gets some assistance from the other side—they will be happy to show up.

27

HEARING YOUR DEPARTED DOG

There is nothing worse than the deafening sound of silence in a home that is suddenly without the pets you love. Personally, I remember one day when I dropped my whole pack off at the groomer and thought of the peace and quiet I was going to get at home for a few hours.

It didn't quite turn out that way because what I discovered was that with my children now adults and out of the house, my fur-kids take their place and give me that feeling of being needed that, as a mother, I long for. They bring the life into our space, the joy into our hearts. When they are gone, it feels empty. I realized that the chaos they bring to our surroundings is also the energy that makes our house feel like a home.

By the time the groomer called to tell me I could pick them up, I was already sitting in her parking lot, impatiently waiting for the phone to ring.

For those of you who only have one pet and, after their loss, have had to return to a silent home, my heart goes out to you. I hope that this chapter can bring you some solace or encourage you to listen for the sounds of your departed pet.

Before it happened to me, I didn't know there were

cases of departed pets being heard audibly. Then, only a few weeks after my Grandpa Oliver died, I recognized his nails clacking against our hardwood floors. I have three dogs, and even from a drowsy state, I can tell which dog is walking without seeing them. Also, Grandpa didn't just walk. He pranced and was the most light-footed dog I've ever heard. It was almost as though he were dancing just on the very surface of the floor.

The night I heard him, I was in bed but hadn't yet gone to sleep. I have insomnia, and it usually takes me two to three hours of lying there with my eyes closed before I drift off. So first I didn't move. Then I realized whose steps I heard, and I sat straight up in bed, looking for my sweet little gentleman.

He wasn't there. But at my feet was Rango, sound asleep as usual. I reached straight under the bed on my side and felt the fur of Riley Radcliffe, as I knew I would, because that is his sleeping place, and he barely moves until the wee hours of the morning.

I lay back against the pillow, at peace in knowing that it was Grandpa.

Of course, being the sponge that I am, I wanted to know if others out there have heard evidence of their pets being around them in spirit. During my research, I found many reports of pet owners hearing the clicking of nails on the floors, their dog's bark, a cat's meow or purr, or even a quiet snore. Sometimes it has been reported that a bell will tinkle, as though it is still on the collar of the animal who is no longer there in body. I can't believe that so many people with thousands upon thousands of reports of their pets coming to them through familiar noises would be delusional or making it up. I believe that yes, your pet may try to come to you from the other side to bring you comfort from your grief.

28

———◆———

THE SCENT OF YOUR DEPARTED DOG

Others have reported witnessing a memorable scent that is an obvious sign their pets are around them. With the keen sense of smell that animals have been given, it is not surprising that they would use a scent to try to tell you hello or get your attention. It could be the smell of their fur, breath, or even their flatulence! (I hope my departed dogs keep that one all to themselves.)

As a side note, when my daughters were young and at home, I was going through a hard time and just getting started with my road to insomnia. One night around midnight, I was getting too deep in my head, thinking of my past and how unloved I had felt. I was missing my grandmother on my mother's side. I think I was having quite a pity party in regard to the rocky relationship between my mother and me.

I was lying on the living room couch and staring at the lamp. Much to my shock, I started smelling the scent of gardenia, which was what my grandmother always wore. I sat up on the couch and looked around then listened for my girls. They were still tucked into bed, as was my husband. I walked around the house and even checked the air spray in the bathroom, confirming it was as far away from the scent of gardenias as you could get.

I finally admitted to myself that it was my grandmother, reminding me that she loved me, and she believed in me, and this was before the feather.

Not to be outdone, more than twenty years later, I was driving down the interstate and thinking of my paternal grandmother. Suddenly I smelled cigarette smoke. And not just any cigarette smoke but the specifically strong scent of Pall Mall cigarettes being smoked.

My grandmother smoked them quite frequently, up until the day of her death from cancer, and I suppose that was the one thing she thought would validate for me that she knew I was thinking of her.

At first, I thought there must be someone smoking in another car nearby, and it was wafting through my vents. However, traffic was bad, and I could see everyone around me and going past me, and I saw no sign of any cigarettes in hand or smoke lingering behind.

I am not a smoker, and my car had never been smoked in.

Literal goose bumps crawled up my arms, which is actually another sign your loved one is around. All that to say, if your dog (or other pet) has departed, and you feel sure you can smell something familiar to them, you are not crazy, and yes, you probably are right.

29

FEELING YOUR DEPARTED DOG

There are only a small number of reports of a pet actually showing themselves in full body or a ghostlike form after they've departed, but it isn't completely unconceivable. Because they are made up of energy, once our pets are gone, it's highly more likely that they are going to use other ways of letting you know they are there. Some of these might be situations where you feel a sudden sense of anxiety and think of them, or you get goose bumps or a shiver.

Some feel ringing in their ears when their pet is visiting, and others report static electricity suddenly around them. If you think about what happens when more energy is in the air, that's what it is like when a spirit is using vibrations to make a visit.

They could even be a shadow that you see from the corner of your eyes that disappears when you try to look straight at it.

Others have asked their pets to send tangible signs and been rewarded with gifts of objects like coins or feathers, usually in unlikely places as to be unusual.

Signs in nature, especially other animals that are known to be sensitive to energy, are used. Butterflies, dragonflies, and birds are common messengers.

Trish, my rescue partner and soul sister, recently lost one of her pack. She and her husband Jerry don't have human children, so their fur-kids are everything to them. After they helped their baby Cocoa Puff in a long battle with kidney disease, they finally made the decision that it was time to let him go and be at peace.

On December 15, with heavy hearts, they were with him until the very last moment as they said their good-byes. The next day, Trish was hit hard with feelings of guilt and doubt that she'd made the right decision.

She was sitting in her living room, drinking coffee and missing her sweet boy. Suddenly, she heard a bird sing-ing loudly—so loud, it sounded like it was literally in her living room with her. She didn't get up to look.

The next morning, she heard the same song and went to the window.

A beautiful scarlet red cardinal was there, singing.

Since then, every morning at the same time, the same—or one identical to it—cardinal has shown up to sing loudly at her window or sitting in the tree closest to her patio.

Despite these signs, by December 23, Trish was still not in a good place and had sunk into such a deep sad-ness that she cried out to the Lord.

"Please, God, please give me a sign that Cocoa is fine and at peace."

A few minutes later, she stepped to the window and looked into the sky, only to feel her spirit soar when she saw an outline in the clouds, a perfect replica of her sweet boy, and it appeared to be chasing a bird.

Cocoa had loved to chase birds in the yard when he was with Trish and Jerry on Earth. Seeing him in the sky gave her hope that her special boy is free of pain and able to chase birds again.

In my research, I found many reports of people seeing the shape of their dogs in the clouds or a glimpse of them from the corner of their eyes, just evidence enough to let them know their pets were still around them.

During the writing of this book while I immersed myself in this subject, my heart has been heavy with missing Grandpa Oliver. At one point, as I was working well into my tenth hour for the day, I heard a sound in the other room and decided to check it out while I got some water.

I passed by Grandpa's framed photo on the wall, and I thought of how it had been a while since he sent me the black butterflies.

At the same time, I thought of my first dog, Czar, and wondered if my parents ever felt like he was around or sent any signs after he died. I was passing our open storm door, and just as I came within view of it, a tiny bird jumped onto the wreath that hung there and peeked in like it was very curious.

Quickly, another bird joined it.

Immediately, without even taking the time to consider it, I felt it was a sign from both dogs.

As if that wasn't enough, the very next day, I was working on this book again but this time doing more research. On Facebook, I found a page that people were talking about connecting with their departed animals. One post I read had a close-up photo of a dog with a ladybug on his nose. I was *literally still reading the post* when suddenly, just above my mouse pad, a tiny ladybug dropped from my desk and landed near my fingers.

In mid-January.

When I had not seen another ladybug for months.

I was so shocked I took a video of the dog/ladybug post, the computer date/time stamp, and the ladybug. Not that I need proof to know why it happened. But it's always nice to show the husband so he doesn't think I've totally lost my mind.

I joke, but there are many of the same sort of events that have happened to people smarter than I am, more esteemed than I am, and of a type that you might not imagine them talking about visits from their departed animals. People with scientific and skeptical backgrounds who cannot reason any other explanation for how it happens.

I have also read many, many reports of someone feeling their dog or other pet in spirit as they jump onto the bed or settle next to them. Many have reported feeling the wetness of their nose against them or a light kiss from a lick or the feeling of them brushing up against their legs.

Those are extraordinary ways that departed animals have been reported to interact with their loved ones. Obviously, it would take you really accepting the possibility and opening yourself up to such a spiritual gift to be able to receive it.

30

———————◆———————

HONORING YOUR DEPARTED DOG

Your animals don't want you to be sad. They loved you unconditionally while they were here on Earth, and they'll continue to do it until you are together again in spirit. To see you happy and comforted was their main goal in life, so don't take that away from them now.

Take the time you need to grieve and know that grief is simply love, not wanting to let go. But eventually, honor them with a smile when you think of them or when you see their photo. Talk to them. Rejoice and give thanks that you were lucky enough to have them in your life, for however long you did.

Reflect over your time with them and pinpoint what their purpose was in being with you. Was there a specific tragic event in your life that they helped you through? Or perhaps they protected you? Once you have decided what their purpose was with you, have a talk with their spirit and thank them for what they did. Go to the places they loved to go with you—special places you hiked together, the dog park, or out on the lake. Anywhere that you took them to give them joy is where you can go again and remember them, and they will be with you.

Lastly, ask your pet for a specific message, just like I did with Grandpa. Keep it simple, so they don't have to expend all of their energy trying to make it happen. Then when you "see" the response to your request—their message—acknowledge it without doubt. Your nod to their efforts will make them happy, and they'll want to do it again.

If you think that it would be an insult to the dog you loved for you to go out and get another dog, you are wrong. Your departed pet wants you to be happy! Finding another companion is not replacing the one that you loved, but I can guarantee that it will give the one that you loved comfort knowing that you are no longer lonely.

A few months after Grandpa died, after some heavy thinking and deliberating, we decided that I would put a deposit on a puppy who had just been born. Obviously, I always recommend rescue, but if you just cannot find the dog that you are longing for, then I also think it is fine to go to a reputable breeder, someone who has references, and you can check them out to make sure that they are not a backyard breeder or a dog hoarder. I did a ton of research, as I am known to do, and found a wonderful woman named Sharon in Tennessee. She had my deposit, and she sent me the picture of a beautiful baby pup I planned to add to our family. I stared at the photo for many, many nights in anticipation.

However, before that dog was ready, a picture of a different pup landed before me. Not a purebred pup of any kind and was probably one of hundreds of pictures that I have seen in groups and on pages, but something in her eyes grabbed hold of me. And though I was going to lose out on my five-hundred-dollar deposit for the other dog, I knew this pup needed me.

I contacted the owner and made arrangements to go and pick her up. To be honest, my Ben didn't feel the same way I did and was not happy with me as I hit the road.

What I found in Tennessee was that the woman was not reputable nor was the puppy healthy and, in my opinion, wasn't even old enough to be away from her mother. The owner claimed that the mother only had the one pup, which was an accident, and the mother refused to let her feed.

When I saw how tiny the pup was, I was really nervous and again questioned her age. The owner declared the pup was almost eight weeks old and healthy, and if I didn't want to take her, she had three backup offers. I knew immediately the dog was not healthy and, if in the wrong hands, would die.

I took the pup, and before I was even half an hour away, I called a reputable breeder friend and told her the situation. She sent me straight to the local PetSmart to get Nutrical and other items, and through a syringe, I fed the pup in the parking lot just to make sure she'd make it to my home.

We headed to the veterinarian the next morning and found out that she weighed less than a pound, had a bad case of coccidia, and was infested with fleas that had depleted her of nutrients.

It would be touch and go whether she would survive or not.

I named her Hazel Beatrix. I've always loved vintage names, and you can't get any more vintage than Hazel. As for her middle name, that is for the famous Beatrix Potter, who began her journey as an author the same way that I did. Helen Beatrix Potter is known mostly for her *Tales of Peter Rabbit* stories, which were modeled after her own bunny, Peter Piper.

Like me, Beatrix loved animals and had quite a menagerie of them around her at all times. In one article, it is said that she would capture wild mice and then let them run loose in her schoolroom.

When Beatrix tried to sell her first book to publishers, she was turned down, so she decided to self-publish it. When I tried to sell my first book to publishers (a memoir called *Silent Tears*), it was turned down, and I self-published it. In essence, we both started our careers by our own determination and tenacity.

Beatrix Potter's books have sold well over ten-million copies and are translated into more than thirty-five languages. While I will likely never reach stardom like that, I am thankful that at the time of this writing, I have sold over a million books and have translations in six languages.

I know, I know… I have a long way to go to catch up, but I've come far from the teenager who left home with a bag of clothes and nothing else.

Sadly, it is also said that despite the great success that Beatrix had, she still felt she was a disappointment to her mother.

Wow—that similarity hits deep.

Back to my own little Beatrix, who we call Hazel Bea. I fed her by syringe, every two to three hours around the clock for the first two weeks then every four to five hours until she was finally able to get through the night.

I never once complained, and as a matter of fact, those feedings were some of the most special moments I've ever had, and I think was a deciding factor in how well we bonded. Once again, I had a dog who needed me as much as I needed them, cradled against my chest in the wee hours of the night as we rocked for comfort.

Despite her deformed little puppy pads that have turned into what her dad calls *bubble feet,* and only three toenails in total, Hazel Bea is now a healthy little girl. She's also everything *I said* I didn't want.

I first declared that I would have a pretty, well-trained dog that I could put bows in her hair and dress in hand-made clothes. My model fur-daughter would be sweet and full of affection and never give me any trouble. I even went on Etsy and into Facebook groups and bought dozens of cute dog dresses and outfits and piles of bows. (I may or may not have even bought her a leather jacket and sunglasses, but do not tell the hubs.) Yes, so I went over the top for a little while there, but cut me a break! I was grieving!

And I'll admit, Hazel Bea can be really sweet, and she gives a lot of affection—but only on her terms. To be honest, she is the sassiest pup I have ever known. Our little tomboy Bea tortures her big brothers Rango and Riley Radcliffe and will not even hear about being put into clothes or having bows in her hair.

The very few times that I have gotten her to dress up have been few and far between with plenty of bargaining done to make it happen.

However, Hazel Bea is quite entertaining as she grabs things she's not supposed to and makes us race around the house to catch her. You should've seen her when I mistakenly laid the Neosporin beside me on the couch while applying to a sore spot on my Ben. Hazel ran with that open tube, her tiny teeth impaling it and squirting it all over the floor as she slid under the couch and around corners in a game of keep-away-from-mommy.

It's also really cute when she interrupts Rango's long naps to infuriate him with kisses. He jerks his head from side to side, trying to avoid the wet slaps she tries to plant on him. At first, he would jump up high where she couldn't reach him, but now she can jump, too, and she loves that she gets him so riled up.

Riley Radcliffe is more forgiving and loves her attention. Together, they chase each other and wrestle in the yard. In his eleventh year, Riley has a new spurt of energy as he tries to keep up with what we now call Hurricane Hazel, or Hazy B when she's feeling her rebellious rapper mood, or even *Dammit Hazel* when she's being ornery.

And talk about a big mush—our little princess has her pack dad wrapped around her little lumpy paw. He took a framed picture of her to work and put it on his desk. That's how crazy he is about her. I'm not sure if it is because he misses his own little girl so much or what the deal is, but suddenly, I hear my tough man in the other room going on and on talking to her, and every night, he kisses her a dozen times before he turns over to go to sleep. It's also entertaining that she takes a shower with him after work every day, coming out with her hair a mess of curls on top from the water. He has tried to keep her out of the bathroom, but she pitches quite a fit as she stands on her back legs and tries to bust through the door. The racket she makes sounds like a grizzly on the other side, and he's found it's easier to just let her in.

She tends to get her way like that.

One day I told him that if something ever happens to me, he'll have to find a good woman to give Hazel Bea to because she needs the full attention of a stay-at-home mom. He looked at me like I was a fool and declared that if something happened to me, he wouldn't let any of our babies go to someone else. I relented and gave him permission to go ahead and remarry, but she has to be a good woman, and first, he has to mourn me for a year.

Anyway, I recently got the courage to give our little hellion another real bath. It's amazing how fast she can become a writhing, uncontrollable creature with snarls and snaps when you try to get her to do something she doesn't want to. Funny thing is, when they are like that, you need to act like their biological parent would and snarl and snap right back. You should see how good I have gotten at baring my teeth and growling just before I nip her in the neck.

I won the bath battle. When I got her out and wrapped her in the towel, all you could see was her little face wet and peeking out. I turned us toward the mirror and was struck speechless with exactly how much she looked like Grandpa probably would've looked when he was a puppy.

I have a gut feeling that he would have had her same sassy personality if I had met him at least a decade before I did. All that to say, there is no doubt in my mind that Grandpa put Hazel Bea's picture in front of me and said, forget about the purebred beautiful girl you thought you wanted because this ball of sass is who you need.

He was right. My heart just explodes with love for Hazel Bea, even in her naughty moments like last week when we got Riley Radcliffe a new bed for his birthday. Hazel Bea was excited when I brought the bed in and kept trying to get in it.

She would hop in, and I'd gently pick her up and take her out.

"No, Hazel Bea, that's Riley's bed," I said. "It's much too big for you."

Then I'd gently pick him up and put him in there.

Hazel argued the point because she thinks that even though she is only five pounds and the boys are seventeen pounds, she is just as big as they are. And she claims all the good stuff.

She ignored me trying to put Riley's stamp of ownership on it and would wiggle right back in there and root him out.

Riley is a lover and not a fighter.

We went through the process multiple times until she gave up.

I thought I won.

The next morning, Hazel Bea was in her tiny bed between Ben and me on our bed. I looked over, and Riley was not in his new bed.

When I went to investigate why, I was ready to spank her tiny bottom (if I was a supporter of spanking!) because she'd gotten the last word. Sometime in the night, she had hopped down and peed all over the inside of the new bed, ensuring that Riley Radcliffe would never claim it as his.

I might've won the first little battle, but she won that war.

Just today, I gave the three of them a small rawhide-free bone. Riley Radcliffe and Hazel Bea snatched theirs up lickety-split, but Rango is always slow, and before he could get it, she grabbed his too!

He looked at me as though to say, "Mommmmm... she took my treat."

"I'll get it, buddy," I said as I chased Hazel Bea around the living room then the bedroom, finally cornering her in the bathroom.

It was hard to believe that her tiny mouth could hold both of those bones, but boy, she could, and she wasn't giving them up without a fight. It took a few, but I finally made her release them, and I took one to her brother.

She glared at me as she chewed on her own beneath my feet at this desk. I have to give it to her. She's a rott-weiler in a little Chorkie body. And even when I scold her, I give her a little wink and a hidden smile, proud of her spunk.

Yes, our Hazel Bea has brought noise to our home and returned joy to our lives again, and I've learned to think of Grandpa with a smile. I miss him, oh so very much, but I also praise God for the short time I had such a wonderful and noble little gentleman to call my own.

Psalms 150:1–6 NIV: "Praise the LORD. Praise God in his sanctuary; praise him in his mighty heavens. Praise him for his acts of power; praise him for his sur-passing greatness. Praise him with the sounding of the trumpet, praise him with the harp and lyre, praise him with timbrel and dancing, praise him with the strings and pipe, praise him with the clash of cymbals, praise him with resounding cymbals. Let everything that has breath praise the LORD."

31

THE RAINBOW BRIDGE

Dog lovers who also believe in Heaven like to find comfort in what is called the Rainbow Bridge. From the research I've done, I have not been able to find any reference in the Bible to a rainbow bridge where the souls of departed dogs gather.

However, God is loving and kind and says we will have "all we desire in His house." Wouldn't it be fair to say that if we are looking forward to a rainbow bridge where all our past dogs wait for us to arrive that God will make sure it's there?

And who knows, He may have seen so much reference to it from all of us here on Earth that He has taken our creative idea, and it is already there and waiting.

As I said in the beginning of this book, there is not any scripture in the Bible that gives a definitive and irrefutable evidence that dogs will be in Heaven. However, God does give us this: "With God, all things are possible" (Matthew 19:26 NIV).

In John 15:7, it says, "If ye abide in me, and my words abide in you, ye shall ask what ye will, and it shall be done unto you." As I read this, I believe it says that if I abide in God (and I do), then what I ask for shall be done. In Heaven, I will ask to see all the people who I have loved and have gone before me, and I will ask the same of my beloved pets.

Because I abide in Him, I feel He will grant my requests.

The Bible also tells us that God made all of creation and put it in paradise on Earth, including the animals, and that it was good (Genesis 1:25). Adam and Eve messed that up for us in the beginning by bringing evil into the world. When paradise is made for all of us again in Heaven after Jesus died for our sins, why wouldn't he include the animals?

If you are wondering why God doesn't speak in the Bible about animals being saved to come to Heaven, it is because they are already saved. Animals are born innocent. It is man that brings evil into the world and must be saved. There is no reason for discussion on saving animals in the teachings of the apostles or God's messages.

Revelation 21:1 says that Heaven is a place where we will enjoy a glorious and perfect version of creation as we already know it. We already know that having our pets with us here on Earth is what makes us happy, so there you go! Also, in Revelation 19:11, it tells us that the "Heavens opened and behold, there was a white horse." In Isaiah 11:6–9, it says, "the wolf also shall dwell with the lamb, and the leopard shall lie down with the kid; and the calf and the young lion and the fatling together; and a little child shall lead them."

If there are horses, wolves, lambs, and leopards in Heaven, why not dogs?

Proverbs 12:10: "A righteous man cares for the needs of his animal." Animals are obviously important to God, or He wouldn't have given us the command to care for them.

And the one that is the deciding factor for me on this entire subject of "do our animals go to Heaven?" is this,

Ecclesiastes 3:19–20: "For what happens to the children of man and what happens to the beasts is the same; as one dies, so dies the other. They all have the same spirit, and man has no advantage over the beasts, for all is vanity. All go to one place. All are from the dust, and to dust all return."

As a Christian, I stand firm in the promise that when I die, I will not remain a pile of unknowing dust without thought, desires, or love. Yes, my body will turn to dust—and that's fine because I hate it anyway—but my soul will be in Heaven. And if my soul is there, according to the scripture above, so will the souls of my dogs. For "they have the same spirit," and "what happens to man will happen to beasts."

If you're a believer in Christ, I don't see how that point can be argued, and an important thing to remember is that God calls us to have faith, in Him and in all things.

In the front of this book, I told you that I would share what I think is my overall lesson in getting through many of my trials in life. I do believe that we all are learning as we traverse the problems and tragedies put in front of us. If I hadn't gone through the tumultuous childhood I did, I wouldn't have such a heart for children in need when I became an adult. With the domestic abuse I survived, I'm able to relate to women from the same situations, as well as put everything I have into making my blessed marriage the best it can be. With all the four-legged therapeutic companions I've known and mentioned here, their presence in my life during the lowest of lows have kept me from being bitter and resentful.

The absolute biggest thing I've learned through everything is simple, really. Many of you have already reached the same conclusion as you look back over your own memories, and some of you will also attribute it to your faith—in God and in animals.

It's to love.

Love hard and love big.

Even when you are in the mire and the deepest trials of your life.

And when faced with the seemingly unlovable.

Just love.

Because love wins.

32

A SEVEN-DAY GRIEF GUIDE

33

DAY ONE OF YOUR GRIEF GUIDE

Today you are hurting so deeply that you think you will never feel joy again. You feel crushed under an all-consuming weight of sorrow. A vital part of your family is gone, and you want them back. Take the time to let your emotions out and acknowledge that to hurt so deeply means that you loved just as deeply, and for that, your pet is thankful. It is okay to grieve, because grief is the price we pay for love.

Some people might feel more angry than sad. If that is you, it's okay to unplug and spend time alone in nature. Take the time to observe that though it was hard, you served your fur-child with dignity and respect in their last moments as they left their physical body. I want you to light a candle as the sun sets across the sky and know that it will light the way for your pet's path to paradise.

Put your pet's tags on your key chain or in a special place. Don't try to move any of their things yet in the home. Leave the toys, bowls, and beds there on this excruciating day. Be kind to yourself. Take heart that in the opinion of those smarter than me that you can be sure your beloved pet is in Heaven.

You might feel like the magnitude of your loss is going unrecognized by those close to you. Or from very insensitive individuals, you might hear things like "just get another one," or "it's a dog, not a child."

First, let me apologize on behalf of their insensitive ignorance. If you feel that you need to talk to someone who understands, the LSU School of Veterinary Medicine has a program called Best Friend Gone that is set up to help those dealing with the loss of a pet. You may reach the Best Friend Gone counselors by calling (225) 578-9547 or by having your veterinarian request that a counselor call you.

Romans 8:19 (KJV): "The lesser creatures await Christ's return to redeem the sons of God so they, too, will be released from physical death to eternal life."

34

DAY TWO OF YOUR GRIEF GUIDE

For today, try to find comfort with someone who understands the magnitude of your loss. If you didn't use the LSU number, do that today if you cannot reach a trusted family member or friend who will not minimize your feelings.

If you do not feel like talking, find an online support group that is specific for those who have lost the best friends that are their animals. Give yourself permission to express exactly how grief-stricken you are, no matter how anyone will judge you.

If you'd like, you are welcome to come to my Facebook page All (my) Dogs Go to Heaven and post a picture and let us all honor them together. Tell us about your pet and how they helped you through life.

Remember that it is normal that you will feel any or all of these emotions: hopeless, lonely, anxious, withdrawn, angry, guilty, and/or fatigued. The only prescription I can give you is time, and even then, you will always miss your best friend.

John 16:24: "So with you: Now is your time of grief, but I will see you again and you will rejoice, and no one will take away your joy."

35

DAY THREE OF YOUR GRIEF GUIDE

Today I want you to go somewhere that you and your pet would go together, like a park or a special trail, or perhaps it was for a ride or even in your own backyard. Find a place that brought them joy and therefore gave it to you as well. Stay there for a time and remember when your pet was full of health and stamina and know that they are out of their earthly body and are light and free. Go back and visit the places your pet loved, for they are with you.

Decide today how you would like to pay tribute to your pet for the gift they were to you. You could scatter their ashes somewhere special or plant a tree in their honor. Some may want to make a donation to a pet rescue in their name. You could even write a letter to your pet expressing your gratitude for all they did for you in your life together.

When my Grandpa pup died, my dad planted a weeping willow tree in our yard for me to place his stone under. The gesture that he acknowledged my deep pain was healing in itself, and I find great solace in watching the tree flourish.

John 14:27: "Peace I leave with you; my peace I give to you. Not as the world gives do I give to you. Let not your hearts be troubled, neither let them be afraid."

36

———◆———

DAY FOUR OF YOUR GRIEF GUIDE

Today it is important for you to change your mind's last visual image of your pet to one of your own choosing. I feel sure that I can say they don't want you to remember them as sick, injured, or lifeless. Go to a quiet place and look at that memory one more time then replace it with a "and then this happened" memory. Imagine the moment their spirit passed over the Rainbow Bridge and through the pearly gates. Who greeted them? Another pet? A family member? Imagine your beloved as strong and healthy, full of joy and anticipation.

Create your moment and hang on to it when you next think of your beloved family fur member. If you have a favorite photo of your pet, send it to an online photo printing company to return it as a framed piece for your home, a reminder of a happier time and of the reunion that is yet to come.

Hang a set of gentle wind chimes near your door so that when you hear them, you can be reminded of your favorite postcard moment you had with your four-legged friend.

Isaiah 40:29: "He gives strength to the weary and increases the power of the weak."

37

_____

DAY FIVE OF YOUR GRIEF GUIDE

Have heart. Your best friend or fur-child is not lost forever. God created animals before He created man, and He delighted in them. When He is ready to restore Heaven and Earth to its previous glory, I am positive that He will include everything that has breath.

Sparrows and dogs are both animals, and Jesus made it clear that God cares for everything of His creation. If He cares so much for sparrows that He knows the path of each and every one of them, I feel assured that He feels the same about the amazing creature of love, protection, and loyalty that we call a dog.

Build or buy a bird feeder and put it where you can see it every day to remind yourself that just as God cares for every feather on the birds' heads, He also loves all his creatures big and small.

Matthew 10:29: "Are not two sparrows sold for a penny? And not one of them will fall to the ground without your Father's will."

38

DAY SIX OF YOUR GRIEF GUIDE

It's the little things that can really bring back the pain, isn't it? The way they followed you around the house or snuggled close to you. The soft snore that sang you to sleep or their excited prance when you walked through the door. Their huge personalities they carried around in small bodies, whether three pounds of sugar or a hundred pounds of loyal muscle, leaves such a lonely place in their wake.

Did you know you can send in a photo of your pet and have it made into a pillow? My soul sister did that for me, and I have found such comfort as I wrap my arms around it and hug my sweet gentleman. The pillows come in different sizes or designs from websites like Etsy, Shutterfly, and others.

Don't feel silly ordering a pillow of your pet. We do what we need to do to get us through, and that's okay. Today, gather your pet's belongings, and if you don't need them, donate to a shelter or a neighbor's pet. Then spend time in prayer and reflect on scripture. Write the following verse on a slip of paper then carry it outside with you for a long walk surrounded by nature.

Psalm 34:18: "The Lord is close to the brokenhearted and saves those who are crushed in spirit."

39

DAY SEVEN OF YOUR GRIEF GUIDE

It's only been a week, and of course, you are still deep in sorrow. You aren't crazy. You aren't silly. You are human. It will take a long time for the pain to subside. Unlike the novels I write, grief doesn't have a plot. There is no beginning or end. My hope is that little by little, you will be able to let go of your grief, though never your love.

If you need to go back through the seven days in the guide, do it as many times as you want. You will always miss your pet, and you may never totally recover from the loss. It's important to acknowledge that you are not moving on. Instead, you are moving forward with your pet still around you in spirit.

At some point, my hope for you is that you will be able to move your weight of grief over to feelings of nostalgia. Why? Because grief is made up strictly of sad memories, but nostalgia is both sad and fond memories together and can help you to recover and remember how blessed you were to have your pet in your life.

Today it would be helpful to write your pet's obituary as a form of therapy and a tribute to the love and loyalty you shared. Make it somber or silly—whatever fits to honor the personality of the creature you miss so terribly. If you are on a social network, post the eulogy along with a photo to help others understand your loss and pay tribute.

Be very aware of the law of threes as it relates to synchronicity. For example, if three times within a matter of days or a week, you hear, feel, smell, or in some other way think your pet is trying to reach out to you to show you they are near, they probably are.

I like this quote about loss and love: "The risk of love is loss, and the price of loss is grief. But the pain of grief is only a shadow when compared with the pain of never risking love." –Hilary Stanton Zunin

Ecclesiastes 3:19–20: "For what happens to the children of man and what happens to the beasts is the same; as one dies, so dies the other. They all have the same spirit, and man has no advantage over the beasts, for all is vanity. All go to one place. All are from the dust, and to dust all return."

When the Bible talks about man and beasts returning to dust, it is my understanding that it's our physical bodies that He refers to. Our spirits will leave that body behind, in the dust, as it soars to the heavens. Be comforted that your beloved pet is in a wonderful place of love and light and is waiting for you on that Rainbow Bridge.

In another time and a happier place, you will meet again.

THE RAINBOW BRIDGE

What is Heaven and the Rainbow Bridge like
A quaint and friendly small town in Heaven
The souls of our pets come sliding down the rainbow
To an entrance of a beautiful field that has a forest on
the far edge
In the warm months shimmering waves of soft heat
Play on strands of meadow grass
A perfect silence marked by an occasional grasshop-
per's hum
The wind whispers carrying sounds of happy animals
The smell is late spring,
Never too hot
In fall a stunning field of gold reds and yellows
Trees vibrant with color
Squirrels heard playing
A chill in the air
A scent of campfire and apples
A winter silent and white
Snow for as far as the eye can see
Falling gently from a steel-gray sky
Twinkly lights adorn trees
A magical feel
Full of vibrant and happy spirit energy
Needs provided as they gain strength
Strength to go on in this beautiful, peaceful place

In the beginning we have few messages
A scent or sign but quick and fleeting
As their energy gets stronger
We will see them in dreams
Or feel them brush by
Signs to bring tears of joy
And to help us grieve
To move forward

Our furry family members will continue to play in the fields of green and in the icy white snow, making new friends daily. They will always have the job of guarding you and your family until you reunite again at the Rainbow Bridge.

Written by Yvonne S.

FROM THE AUTHOR

Thank you for reading *All (my) Dogs Go to Heaven*. I hope you have enjoyed reading a little about my life, the dogs who have brought me comfort, and what led me to do this research. It is my hope that sharing this book with all of you will do some small part in helping you with the sorrow of losing your beloved furry family member.

Please know that while you may feel alone in your grief that throughout the world, there are other pet parents who have been where you are and know your loss. To any of you who have had your own experience with a departed pet and would like to tell me about it for consideration of adding it to a Volume II of this book, please email me as many details as possible, and some photos, to kay@kaybratt.com.

I have one more small story to share with you, that came about on the day I finalized all the edits in this book and victoriously called it done. I heard a small noise in the other room, but when I looked around my office, all three of my pups were with me. I went to investigate, and it took me a while to figure it out, but finally when I had just about given up and was returning to my office, I passed the standing bookshelves where I have Grandpa's ashes, his hat, and his tiny pawprint made in plaster.

The round plaster disc with his paw print had fallen

forward, laying face down in front of the small box of his ashes.

Yes, Grandpa, we did it. It is done and we have told your story, my sweet, sweet little gentleman. No one will ever be able to convince me that he wasn't the one who gave me the words I needed to share with all of you.

Again, I appreciate each and every reader and want you to know that a portion of any profits from this book will go toward dog rescue. If you enjoyed ALL (my) DOGS GO TO HEAVEN, I would be very thankful if you would leave a customer review on your preferred platform to help raise visibility of the book. Tell me about your own pet in the review, for I would be honored to hear it.

If you would like to read more about dogs, my book WISH ME HOME is a novel about a young woman who sets off on a journey and meets a homeless dog along the way. It's a fan favorite, and here is what one reader had to say:

I just finished Wish Me Home *last night and I fell in love with all the characters Kay created. To prove that this was a great read, when I turned the last page, I rolled over and gave my pup a hug and to her credit, she uttered a satisfied sigh knowing I had enjoyed it very much.*

–Reviewed by a pet-loving reader like you

Another Kay Bratt novel called DANCING WITH THE SUN is a story of a mother and daughter who find themselves lost in more ways than one. If you believe in symbolism from the other side, I think you will enjoy it. Carolyn Brown, the New York Times bestselling author, called it "A baring-of-the-soul emotional story that leaves you with a heart full of love and hope."

For a complete list of my book titles, including series and reading orders, please find my website https://kay-bratt.com. Also, if you'd like to receive my monthly newsletter, you will get news of my just-released books, sales, and lots of fun giveaways for my readers. I also give you anecdotes of the goings-on and escapades of my Bratt Pack.

You can sign up here: https://www.subscribepage.com/kaybrattnewsletter, but if you prefer not to subscribe, you can also hit the Follow button on my author page to simply be alerted when a new Kay Bratt novel is released.

With gratitude,
Kay of the Bratt Pack

ACKNOWLEDGMENTS

My heartfelt gratitude goes to contributors to this book as follows. Dexter's mom, Laurie. Belle's mom, Suzette. Cocoa's mom, Tricia Flippin, RN, BSN to humans and volunteer for Yorkie Rescue of the Carolinas. Author Tammy Grace, who also writes about the bond we have with dogs. Yvonne S, Makita's mom, and Errol Green, dad to Scooby. A big thanks to artist Ken Robinson for the portrait of Hazel Bea looking up at Grandpa in Heaven. Ken uses traditional canvas and brush along with digital technology to create custom paintings. Specializing in animal portraits, Ken works from client photos, producing outstanding and original works of art. Contact Ken to commission your pet's portrait at www.expresspetportraits.com.

I'm also sending love and gratefulness to my pets waiting for me at the Rainbow Bridge, including Grandpa Oliver, Czar, Paco, Ethel, Sam, Grandpa, Max, Milo, Boomer, and others. To my pack still here on Earth, Riley Radcliffe, Runaway Rango, Kamikaze Kaiser, Griffy Boy, Gypsy, and Hazel Bea, thank you for loving me so completely. To the many critters who have left paw prints in my home and on my heart, thank you for letting me play a small part in helping you find a home again: Griffin, Lola, Primrose, Noodles, Bella Blu, Clarabelle, Bailey, Stewey, and Chi Chi.

The members of my Krew know who they are, but

I'm not sure they know how much they mean to me and how their support keeps me going when the going gets rough. Thank you all for supporting my work and my frequent tendency to bare my soul. Thank you for helping me with all the acts of kindness over the years, especially those related to dogs who find their way onto my path. I hope you always stay within my circle of trusted friends.

To my good friends, Alice Lynn and Doug Stein, my gratitude is yours forever because you accepted our sweet girl, Gypsy, into your home and your hearts, and have given her the best retirement she could ask for.

To a dear friend who came into my life recently at a time that I most needed, thank you to infinity. In Greek history, a cardinal is considered the birds of the sun and thought that when singing their song, even the sun would stop to listen. Their tune has a quality that is uplifting and fills our souls, giving us rejuvenation and strength when we need it most. I will forever think of you when I hear the cardinal sing and remember that with your counsel, you brought me through some of my darkest days.

To my daughters, who I love very much. I hope you'll read this book one day and know that I never gave up trying to be a better person than I was probably meant to be. When you go through the hard times—and feel that things can't get darker—please remember to keep fighting so that you can also find your happily ever after. To my beloved grandchildren, you have brought me so many smiles and so much joy to my heart. I love you.

Many of us find our comfort within our online community, and I want to thank the following for the welcoming and comforting atmospheres in Facebook groups they've created for dog lovers like me to come. Skipper Neuzerling in the Crazy Yorky Ladies and Dudes, Nancy Cameron Iannios in Yorkie Addiction,

Barbara Kowalski in Traveling Yorkies R Us, Sonya Barto in The Yorkie Club, William Thomas in the Chorkie Owners Club, and Barb and Ed Beck in Living a Yorkie Life.

To Judy Morgan and Tricia Flippin of Yorkie Rescue of the Carolinas, thank you for being my close friends and rescue partners and allowing me to share in the joy of bringing happily fur-ever afters to dogs who deserve it the most.

Judy Morgan, Tricia Flippin, and I also want to thank some of our favorite rescuers who have opened their homes and hearts (and wallets) to our Yorkie Rescue of the Carolina's pups: Kimberly Moore and Wayne Jackson, Jaime Angeles and Gary Heying, Kristin Quinlan, Debbie Nelson, Sheila Maserick, Erin Camacho, Audrey Curlee, Carolyn Homoly, Erin Mathena, Eddie and Tara Lewis, Ashley Dodson and Tosha Champ with TLC Grooming, Jim and Kathie Huff, Jessica Seel, Debbie Blume, Didi Harmon, Donna McBryar, Kirsten Zimmerman, Tina Varney, Mark and Cindy Wentzel, Kristy Burgess, Cheryl Smith, Rebecca Venderklok, Leslie Morgan, Cheryl Kaufman, Dana Hughes, Chris Hayes, Jo Montgomery, Cheri Smith, Crystal Huff, Michael Drolet and Jimmie Dillon, John Howard, Mona Ghali Green, Anita Haney Lee, Taryn Noël, Jessie Lanier, Micheke Homier, Deb Fortenberry, Shannon Norrie, Shannon Griepsma, Mary Clay, Ruth Ward, Cynthia Bellacero, Nancy Owens, Kelly Ozgunduz, Sherry Arant and Ross Vance, Debbie and Mike Nelson, Andrea Mahoney, Larry and Dianne Deewaard of Yorkie Fashion Fantasy, Deborah Johnston, Donna Musselwhite, Cheryl Smith, Jessica Seel, Kirsten Swackhamer, Evelyn Johnston, Debbie Lyerly, Dina Eagles, Tracy Baker, Sheri and Ben Woodruff, Debra Himsel, Evelyn Johnson and so many more. I wish I could name you all but please know everything you do to foster, adopt, and support is very much appreciated and makes you part of our YROC family.

To my parents who I am lucky are still living, thank you for all that you did to keep us together as a family. You both went through some very hard times, yet you never once considered your children as burdens. Now that I've lived long enough for my own children to start adding up my faults, I realize that you were both doing the best you could, and that was enough. I hope you see that I'm doing the best I can as a daughter, and give me grace. And as long as I'm making wishes, I wish that you would forgive each other and come together in peace, for your family.

To my siblings, I love you and I'm sorry that we've all learned to fight our demons separately, and cannot come together to heal.

Lastly, I can't skip acknowledging my amazing husband, Ben, for all that he does to help me in the sometimes-chaotic life of a trauma-surviving-dog-loving-rescue-author lady. It only took two decades to bring him over to the dog side and get him to fully embrace being a certified card-carrying dog parent who hurries home because he feels guilty for leaving the pack alone for too long. In addition to helping me keep the Bratt Pack fed, cuddled, and walked, he is now my partner in crime for delivering warm doghouses, beds, treats, and toys to random strangers' dogs, and that alone proves I picked the right prince.

Or—*he picked me.*

ABOUT THE AUTHOR

Kay and Riley Radcliffe at Windy Hill

As a writer, Kay uses writing to help her navigate a tumultuous childhood, followed by nearly a decade of abuse as an adult. After working her way through the hard years, Kay emerged a survivor and a pursuer of peace—and finally found the courage to share her stories. She is the author of novels published by Lake Union Publishing and under her own label. Kay writes women's fiction and historical fiction, and her books have fueled many exciting book club discussions and sold more than a million copies around the world.

Kay's work has been featured in Women's World, Adoption Today Magazine, Southern Writer's Magazine, Shanghaiist, Suzhou Sojourner, Historical Novels Society, Anderson Today, and Bedside Reading. Her books have been recommended on LitChat, BookRiot, Midwest Review, Inside Historical Fiction, Blogcritics, The Shawangunk Journal, and Between the Lines (Atlanta, NPR). Her works have been translated into German, Korean, Chinese, Hungarian, Czech, and Estonian.

As a rescuer, Kay currently focuses her efforts on animal rescue and is the Director of Advocacy for Yorkie Rescue of the Carolinas. As a child advocate, she spent a number of years volunteering in a Chinese orphanage, as well as providing assistance for several nonprofit organizations that support children in China, including An Orphan's Wish (AOW), Pearl River Outreach, and Love Without Boundaries. In the USA, she actively served as a Court Appointed Special Advocate (CASA) for abused and neglected children in Georgia and spearheaded numerous outreach programs for underprivileged children in the South Carolina area.

As a wanderer, Kay has lived in more than four dozen different homes, on two continents, and in towns and states from coast to coast in the USA. She's traveled to Mexico, Thailand, Malaysia, China, Philippines, Central America, Bahamas, and Australia. Currently, she and her soul mate of more than twenty-five years enjoy life in their forever home on the banks of Lake Hartwell in Georgia, USA.

Kay has been described as southern, spicy, and a little sassy. Social media forces her to overshare, and you don't want to miss some of the antics that goes on with her and the Bratt Pack. Find her on Facebook, Twitter, and Instagram, and then buckle up and enjoy the ride.

HOME REMEDIES FOR DOGS

If you are reading this book in preparation for the hard day that will be coming with your pet, and you'd like some advice on home remedies for those difficult days leading up, see below. Thank you to Tricia Flippin, RN, BSN to humans and volunteer for Yorkie Rescue of the Carolinas, for this detailed list of home remedies.

Disclaimer: The following is not meant to be certified medical advice. Please check with your veterinarian for approval before using any listed remedies or recipes in this published work.

For Pain: CBD oil for dogs. (I use Lazarus Naturals. They offer both a full spectrum CBD and a THC-free CBD for pets that is taste free, as well as CBD treats, all of which are great products for anxiety and/or pain relief.)

Pet Wellbeing Comfort Gold is also a good product for pain relief. I give this to my elderly dog, Peanut, with Manuka honey in the mornings and mixed with CBD, Nutrical, and a probiotic at bedtime. He has arthritis and dementia, and the combination helps him tremendously.

Mouth or Stomach Ulcers/Reflux: Fresh cabbage juice. (Finely chop cabbage, add filtered water, and bring to a boil. Reduce heat and simmer for fifteen minutes. Strain and cool. Administer one cc to side of mouth with syringe at bedtime.) Juice will keep in the fridge for a couple days. You want it to be fresh, so only make a little bit at a time.

Diarrhea: Nutramax Proviable KP Paste with Proviable DC capsule sprinkled and mixed together. (You can buy these two products together in a kit.)

Tummy Issues/Reflux/Constipation: Slippery elm in coconut water. I use Natures Answer Slippery Elm capsules. Open the capsule and sprinkle a little into about two cc of natural coconut water.

Natural Antibiotic/Energy/Overall Health: Manuka honey.

Appetite Stimulant/Vitamins/Energy/Add Weight: Nutri-Cal is a great supplement to keep on hand for times when your baby needs extra nutrients and calories.

Pre and Probiotic: Nutramax Proviable-DC Capsules. Open capsule and sprinkle into two cc coconut water daily.

Probiotic/Add Weight: Stonyfield organic whole milk yogurt. (Some dogs do not tolerate dairy products.) For those who can, this is a great way to add extra calories to frail, underweight dogs.

You can use these products in any combination you choose. I have found that two oz. stainless steel sauce cups are perfect to mix fur baby supplements in. It is also handy to get a box of one cc syringes, so you always have some on hand to administer supplements.

For Skin and/or Ear Rashes: Colloidal silver. (Sovereign Silver Bio-Active Silver Hydrosol liquid and Silver Miracles Colloidal Silver Gel are very good products.)

For Diarrhea: Rice water will help firm up stool. (Boil white rice, drain water, and cool; offer to dog to drink. Mix with a little bit of plain chicken or beef broth to make it more enticing. Or give one to two cc via syringe. Repeat as needed.)

*Amounts given for all of the recommended supplements are for small dogs (five to ten lbs.). Amounts may be increased for larger dogs.

Tummy Soothing Meal or Snack Recipe:

(Make ahead and freeze in desired portions.)

2 cups boiled chicken or cottage cheese
2 cups steamed rice,
1/3 cup pumpkin
1 Tbsp. Slippery Elm powder

Add some plain yogurt or probiotic powder and water just before serving.

SLOW COOKER DOG FOOD RECIPE

I f your pet is not interested or not able to handle commercial dog food at this time, you may want to experiment with cooking their meals. One rule of thumb from a veterinarian recommendation is to keep your recipes to the following balance:

Sixty percent protein can be chicken thighs and/or breasts with the skin, chicken livers, ground chicken breasts, or ground turkey. Twenty percent vegetables can be sweet potato, pumpkin, carrots, or potatoes. Twenty percent oatmeal or rice. Canine nutritional supplement.

Disclaimer: The following is not meant to be based on certified medical advice. Some dogs require a diet of smaller amounts of protein due to illness. Please check with your veterinarian for approval before using any listed remedies or recipes in this published work.

KAY BRATT'S CONCOCTION
Ingredients

2 1/2 pounds ground turkey breast or ground chicken

1 1/2 cups basmati rice

1 (15-ounce) can sodium-free kidney beans, drained and rinsed

1 1/2 cups chopped butternut squash

2 cups chopped carrots or fingerlings

1/2 cup peas, frozen or canned

4 cups water, or 3 cups water, and 1 can organic chicken broth

Optional to add a canine nutritional supplement like fish oil or other

Drain and rinse all vegetables. Dump everything into a slow cooker. Cover and cook on low for 5–6 hours, stirring as needed. Freeze what cannot be eaten within five days. (Try freezing in muffin tins!) What I like to do is add a bit of warm water to 1/3 cup of concoction to make it a bit soupy before serving. For my big boys, they get this over their kibble. Can be a solo meal, though.

*Please note that brown rice is not recommended for dogs, according to the American Kennel Club. It's much harder on a dog's digestive system. Basmati rice is easier on the gastrointestinal system of dogs. Rice is a fast-digesting carbohydrate, so there's a chance it will cause your dog's blood sugar to rise and is only recommended after veterinarian approval. Healthy snack options for your dog can include (small doses) blueberries, apple, watermelon, green beans, bananas, and broccoli.

Printed in Great Britain
by Amazon

14116982R00140